HOW
TO WOR
EFFECTIV

HOW TO WORK EFFECTIVELY

THE SECRET OF SUCCESS
IN YOUR JOB

NEC & Lucas

THORSONS PUBLISHING GROUP

First published 1985 by National Extension College, Cambridge, for Lucas Open Learning, Solihull.

Designed by Vicky Squires, cartoons by Amanda McPhail.
The Publishers wish to thank Sperry Ltd for permission to quote from their leaflet, *Your Listening Profile*.

British Library Cataloguing in Publication Data

Pates, Andrew
How to work effectively.
1. Work. Organisation.
I. Title II. Blackwell, John
306'.36

ISBN 0 7225 17637

Published by Thorsons Publishers Limited, Wellingborough, Northamptonshire NN8 2RQ, England.

Printed in Great Britain by Mackays of Chatham, Kent.

10   9   8   7   6   5   4   3   2   1

CONTENTS

INTRODUCTION

The aim of this book

This book is a simple guide to overcoming the problems that get in the way at work. It therefore covers the age-old problem of how to fit all the things we have to do into twenty four hours, how to handle those knotty problems that always crop up, how to store things so that we can find them when we need them and at the end of the day – how to switch off.

It is not, however, a book of management theory nor a work of psychology or sociology; while borrowing some ideas from all these fields it is essentially a book based on everyday experience, written with a minimum of jargon and applying principles of common sense to everyday problems.

Who this book is for

The authors have written this book for anybody who works in whatever field (and that can mean doing a job, running a voluntary organisation, pursuing a hobby etc). It will be particularly helpful to those people who have to organise a large part of their own work such as managers and supervisors in industry or commerce, people who run their own business or anybody who has to do more than a purely repetitive and mechanical job.

How to use this book

Each of the eight chapters has the same structure. Every chapter:

- takes a theme (listed in the contents – above)
- outlines the key issues
- gives examples of how those issues affect work
- suggests ways of handling the issues, in some cases with examples of what happened when other people used the approach.

Each chapter is self-contained and can be read by itself, though they do of course relate to one another. Throughout the text you'll find symbols alerting you to key features, all of which are designed to help make your learning as effective – and enjoyable – as possible. The symbols used, and the features they alert you to are as follows:

At the beginning of each chapter

Indicates a list of objectives – key activities that you should be able to carry out when you have completed the chapter. You'll find a reminder at the end of each chapter to check back over this list.

Within each chapter

reminds you that we are about to ask you to carry out a written activity - either in the text itself or, if you prefer, in a separate notebook. We strongly recommend that you find someone to discuss your answers with – perhaps someone who is also using this book. We'll refer to this person as your adviser.

indicates that we are asking you to do something. This may simply be to think about an issue or idea, or it may involve you in a practical activity, say, recording your progress at work over several days. The same symbol is also used against *checklists*, which you may wish to cut out or photocopy and refer to in future.

indicates an example – say, of someone else's work methods or of a real-life problem that someone has encountered.

You may not find it easy to discuss your own effectiveness at first - but once you've broken the ice you'll find it well worthwhile. So try to find someone you already feel at ease with, and aim to keep your discussion as informal as possible. The activity on p 12 will be a good point at which to try out this approach for the first time.

At the end of each chapter

suggests a personal agenda for action – a set of resolutions to put what you have learnt into practice. This is a reminder that the book is about practical, attainable changes in working habits. One way of recording your agenda is as an 'action plan' – a list of targets with a date for the attainment of each. Here are some typical entries from one such plan:

● Reduce overtime costs by 40 per cent by 31/10

● Eliminate stock discrepancies by improving the system of stock control by Christmas break

● Improve the understanding of their job among my four supervisors by preparing job descriptions with them by 15/8

● Get flow of copy to the composing room on agreed schedules by 25/7

There is also a summary of objectives for the whole book on pages 6-7.

If you decide that you have not achieved what you set out to do:

● discuss the objectives with someone – preferably your adviser. Have you interpreted these correctly? Have you set out to do too much too soon?

● work through the relevant section of text again, taking particular note of the practical steps we recommend

● above all, persist: if the objective is one you value the effort you put into achieving, it will be well worthwhile.

In addition, each chapter ends with:

● a short 'signpost' list of related material in other chapters.

● a list of possible sources of help that you might use in your own workplace.

The authors

Andrew Pates is a training consultant and author of several books on education and training for adults, and on job change and career development. He has previously worked in a range of industries.

John Blackwell was for many years Training Manager in a large company and used and developed many of the techniques described in this book. He is now Training Adviser based at the National Extension College.

The examples

The examples of particular issues, problems and ways of doing things are based on real examples from a range of industries. The book has also been piloted at draft stage by people in a variety of jobs, with varying levels of responsibility. Their comments have led to modifications which should ensure that the text is fully in touch with your practical needs - whatever your job or working environment.

CHAPTER OBJECTIVES

Use this list as an overview of *How to Work Effectively*. If your time is limited you may find it helpful to take chapters in order of priority and work through them in that order. If you have only *very* limited time, select just the chapters whose objectives match your immediate needs and concentrate first on these. You can then return to further chapters when the opportunity arises.

CHAPTER 1 – YOU AND YOUR JOB

After reading this chapter you will be able to:

- identify areas of your job in which you could develop further
- use your job description effectively
- outline the key result areas in your job
- review your performance regularly.

CHAPTER 2 – THE RIGHT TASK AT THE RIGHT TIME

After reading this chapter you will be able to:

- review how you use your time at present
- organise your use of time more effectively
- identify ways in which you can avoid wasting time
- achieve your time plans.

CHAPTER 3 – WHEN THE GOING GETS TOUGH

After reading this chapter you will be able to:

- predict routine problems in your work
- cope with unexpected problems
- handle problems effectively.

CHAPTER 4 – YOU AND YOUR WORKPLACE

After reading this chapter you will be able to:

- identify the factors in your working environment which can affect efficient working
- suggest beneficial changes that could be made in your own environment
- get such changes made.

CHAPTER 5 – WORKING WITH PEOPLE

After reading this chapter you will be able to:

- explain what makes a team work
- delegate more effectively
- identify which of your communication skills you would like to improve.

CHAPTER 6 – FOR EVERYTHING, A PLACE

After reading this chapter you will be able to :

- explain the importance of storing things systematically
- organise the things you use at work
- find things when you need them.

CHAPTER 7 – COPING WITH CHANGE

After reading this chapter you will be able to:

- identify the changes that are happening which affect the way we work
- consider the key changes in your own work
- make some changes yourself.

CHAPTER 8 – SWITCHING OFF

After reading this chapter you will be able to:

- pinpoint the sources of stress in your work
- organise your work so that you can minimise stress
- prepare a plan to lead a less stressful life
- switch off!

1: YOU AND YOUR JOB

 When you have completed this chapter you wil be able to:

- identify areas of your job in which you could develop further
- use your job description effectively
- outline the key result areas in your job
- review your performance regularly.

INTRODUCTION

How often are you very busy, so busy you don't have time to stop and think? And don't you sometimes feel that you are not achieving all that you want, that the *activity* you are engaged in is in fact taking up all your time, perhaps even to the extent that it fails to lead to the *results* you want. This can happen at home, at work – anywhere where you are trying to achieve things, though for most of us it is at work that it probably matters most.

You may feel frustrated because you aren't achieving what you want to achieve without knowing WHY; you may know *why* but still not know what to do about it.

You may feel frustrated ...

The key theme throughout the book, is how to make the INPUTS in your job that will achieve the OUTPUTS you require. This chapter starts our discussion about improving effective working by looking at the two key elements in the process, namely:

- YOU AND
- YOUR JOB.

YOU

We are all used to analysing ourselves – we do it when we apply for jobs in the form of a curriculum vitae (CV) or résumé, a letter of application or in the job interview itself – but very often we stop looking at ourselves once we've got the job, maybe once the interview is over, the job offer received or the contract signed. After all, having focused so hard on getting the job, putting all our skill into proving how suitable we were for the post, we have now achieved our goal – we can relax!

But it is precisely at this moment that we should sharpen up our skills and apply them to the job in question; once the job application is behind us we come face-to-face with the demands of the job itself. Our application may have taken several weeks, or even months, but the job itself will usually involve us much longer, maybe for a very long time. It will determine how much time and money we have and if we perform effectively our life will be much easier and more satisfying. After all, our time is precious, our productive time even more so, to our employer, and to the wider world.

The problem is that what happens in a job application is essentially a *backward* look at ourselves. What is needed for effective performance is a *forward* look at where we are going and how we can get there.

You may have a CV or résumé that you have used recently for a job application. Most people put this away after getting a job and forget about it until next time. It's at least as useful however, as a way of monitoring where you're going. When used in this way it is labelled The Dynamic CV to denote that it's continually changing (a reflection of you) in contrast to the static one which is only brought out and dusted down on special occasions.

The Dynamic CV

What do you bring to your work? You can start to compile your dynamic CV in the same way you write any CV – by listing things you've done (like jobs and courses), qualifications you've obtained, things you've achieved and so on. But these all provide the backward look. To look ahead we need to add:

- A list of your strengths, for example that you're good at devising systems.

- A list of your weaknesses, for example that you don't know as much as you'd like about how new technology affects your work.

- Your personal growth points, for example that you have the motivation, time and energy to learn a foreign language and that this has all sorts of implications for the way you might develop your work and your leisure time.

- Where you want to go, for example that you would like to run your own department within two years.

Strengths

What are the things you are good at, the skills you bring to different situations, your personal assets? These will probably show up in the things you have achieved already.

Weaknesses

Where are you *less* competent than you would like to be? This might include things you dislike about yourself, or skills which you feel you might lack. They could be things that have held you back from achieving your goals.

A weakness is seen by many people as something negative about themselves; it can however also be helpful if we identify it and recognise it as an area for development.

In overcoming a weakness you can achieve a great leap forward in your work.

Personal Growth Points

These indicate ways in which you could develop, using the experience, skills and knowledge you have, or might soon acquire.

Where Do You Want To Go?

There is no point in identifying points for growth if you don't *want* to go in that direction. It is important to take your personal preferences into account. Acting effectively is very difficult if you (or someone else) are trying to push yourself in a direction you don't want to go!

WHERE ARE YOU GOING?

Now complete these statements to find out more about where you are going in your job.

My strengths are:	I can develop them further by:	Do I want to do so?
_____	_____	_____
_____	_____	_____
_____	_____	_____
_____	_____	_____

My areas of weakness are:	I can change them by:	Do I want to do so?
_____	_____	_____
_____	_____	_____
_____	_____	_____
_____	_____	_____

How far can I use my strengths to better effect?_____

Does changing my weak areas open up any possibilities?_____

My growth points are: _____

Where do I want to be in:

- six months?

- two years?

- five years?

If possible discuss your answers with an adviser, as we suggested in the introduction.

Check:

- how far your own view of your strengths and weaknesses corresponds to *their* view of them

- whether you have been realistic about your own aims and potential

eg HERE'S WHAT A TECHNICAL WRITER SAID

My strengths:

I'm good at having ideas.

I'm good (and experienced) at turning ideas into products and at bringing order to a mass of ideas and material.

I'm good at devising systems.

I'm meticulous and careful in the jobs I do.

I have a wide knowledge of my field.

I'm good at presenting information to people in face-to-face situations too.

I'm a good listener.

My weaknesses:

I work slowly.

I work over pedantically – I'm not good at separating unimportant detail from crucial action.

I underestimate the time I need to do a job.

I can't write in a literary style.

I'm timid – scared of going off into the unknown.

I don't share work well and don't delegate easily.

My growth points are:

In applying my knowledge and organisational skills to running a department.

In applying my skills to fields outside my technical area, in order to provide broader working horizons.

I therefore need to:

- develop my managerial skills
- pace my work better.

In six months I could hope to run my own department.

In one year I would like to have produced some material to a publishable standard, for someone outside my immediate field.

You are now beginning to map out a plan for action. You might want to use this to:

- make your CV more forward-looking when applying for another job
- to focus on your present work.

YOUR JOB

If asked what their job involves, many people would probably refer to their job description; if you have one, this section will help you to decide how useful it is. If you *don't* have one – the whole of this section could be useful both to yourself and to your employer. Even if you are self-employed, it's useful to sit down once in a while and to ask 'just exactly what *is* my job?'

14

A Poor Job Description

Many job descriptions are merely a list of things we're expected to do. This may be a useful starting point but it is not enough because:

- it doesn't help you sort out priorities
- it doesn't provide goals
- it doesn't indicate how you should evaluate your performance.

In other words, it is written in terms of inputs not outputs.

A Good Job Description

A good job description looks at the 'what' of the job, not the 'how'. It is not an operations manual. An effective job description should have several distinct themes:

1. the purpose of the job
2. key result areas
3. measures of success
4. ways of checking progress
5. in some jobs, a review period for the job description itself.

In a large organisation, there may be more than one layer to a job description; there may well be a general one that applies to all staff at a particular level, supplemented with more detailed ones for specific jobs.

Here are some examples of good job descriptions followed by more detailed notes about each of the five themes above.

15

JOB DESCRIPTION FOR AN ADMINISTRATIVE POST

Position: Centre Administrator

Department: Training Centre, South East Region.

Responsible to: Training Manager, South East Region.

Overall Purpose of Job: To provide administrative support for conducting the Centre's training events; to run its accounting system and to provide secretarial services for the full-time and part-time staff of the Centre.

Training Events:
(a)   Receive enrolments for training events and issue joining instructions.
(b)   Arrange venues and ensure that training aids are available as required.
(c)   Receive reports and statistical information on training events.
(d)   Maintain a record of all national and regional training events together with information on participants as required by the Company.

Finance/Budgets:
(a)   Review and process all invoices concerned with the Centre's purchases.
(b)   Maintain accounts records of all expenditure.
(c)   Prepare monthly claims statistics and forms for submission to the Finance Department.
(d)   Review and check all claims for payment from Associate and Consultant Trainers prior to settlement.
(e)   Maintain a continuous review of actual expenditure against budget.

Administration:
(a)   Type letters, handouts and course literature for the Centre's full and part-time staff.
(b)   Organise, develop and maintain the Centre's filing system.
(c)   Prepare and distribute mailings on the Centre's events and activities.
(d)   Order and maintain adequate stocks of stationery.

Relationships:
This position calls for the maintenance of effective working relationships with the staff of the national and regional Training Departments, the Centre's Consultant and Associate Trainers, other departments in the company which use the training facilities from time to time, the Finance Department and the Centre's suppliers.

Deadlines to Meet:
(a)   Ensure that joining instructions are notified to course participants at least ten days before the training event.
(b)   Render monthly financial and attendance returns according to schedule.
(c)   Ensure adherence to the provision of monthly claim statistics to the Company.

Occasional Duties: Represent the Centre at promotions and public events as requested by the Regional Training Manager.

JOB DESCRIPTION FOR A MANAGERIAL POST

<u>Role:</u> Factory Management.

<u>Outline:</u>
Plans and achieves short- and long-term output levels required to meet customer demand through control of manufacturing resources and services.

- Plans and controls production resources to ensure that the required levels of output, meeting varying customer requirements and agreed quality standards, are achieved at minimum cost.
- Organises purchasing and factory supply activities to obtain the economic sourcing and timely availability of materials to ensure production continuity.
- Directs and integrates production related engineering services to ensure the availability of efficient manufacturing facilities and resolve production problems.
- Ensures that adequate manning levels are maintained and suitable manpower resources are recruited and trained within agreed budget. Reviews and introduces up-dated incentive payment schemes to ensure maximum utilisation of the labour force.
- Becomes actively involved in the preparation of financial forecasts for the ongoing business major projects and new product introductions.
- Undertakes budgetary reviews to meet changing requirements and circumstances.
- Is involved in policy, planning, financial and organisational decisions to meet business objectives.
- Ensures that statutory and company regulations are observed.
- Becomes involved in industrial relations discussions and negotiations including appeals pro cedures at advanced stage.
- Determines requirements and obtains plant and tools to meet forecast customer demand.
- Coordinates the satisfactory introduction of new and modified products.
- Responsible for personnel management, including motivation, development and succession to maintain the operational effectiveness of the function.

Dimensions

Sales turnover	£
Output at cost	£
Workforce (total):	
Manual	
Administrative	
Value of materials	£
Stockholding (gross)	£
'Live' product types:	
Number of customers:	
Department budget	£
Subordinates	

The point about each of these descriptions is that they are:

● absolutely specific. A good job description avoids generalisations and vague references. It's better to err on the side of length than of brevity.

● clearly set out. These descriptions have not been scribbled down in five minutes. Their writers have taken the trouble to plan them out for maximum clarity. Well-chosen headings enable us to locate specific points at a glance.

● actively expressed. Note the verbs that have been used: review, type, direct, coordinate. An effective job description uses these 'hard' verbs in preference to 'soft' ones such as 'understand' or 'be aware of'. Why? because active phrases express measurable, observable events, invaluable for monitoring and reviewing performance.

1. Job Purpose

Jot down notes in answer to the following:

What is your company (or organisation) about?
What is the purpose of running the business?
What is the purpose of your department within the business?
What is the underlying purpose of your job?
Why does it exist?
What would happen if it did not exist?

2. Key Result Areas

Note down:
- your roles
- who you report to
- who reports to you
- what budget or money you have to account for or have the power to spend.

3. Measures of Success

A measure of success is simply a goal together with a note of what you have to do to achieve it.

Note down:
- your overall goals
- the key results that you have to achieve
- the deadlines you have to meet
- activities that recur regularly
- problems you have to overcome frequently.

To decide on the satisfactory level of performance for each of these goals write a list of the outcomes that you would like to see in your job:
- in an hour
- in a day
- in a week

and so on.

You should end up with a set of statements for each of your key results. Since these are so important, we discuss them further below.

Key Results

Your key results must relate to the goals of the business as a whole. You can classify them in terms of:

● OUTPUT: what you do 'to', 'for' or 'about' the goods or services with which your company or organisation is involved.

● FINANCE: budget, cost, profit and/or revenue responsibilities.

● STAFF/EMPLOYEE RELATIONS.

● COMMUNICATION/LIAISON: what you need to do to get maximum support from people both inside and outside the organisation.

● PLANT/BUILDING/EQUIPMENT.

● STATUTORY REQUIREMENTS.

● MARKETS/CUSTOMERS/SALES.

● INNOVATION.

Here, as a guide, is a selection of key results from different jobs. Note that, as in the examples we gave earlier, they all start with an active verb, i.e: a word to describe what someone has to do.

- Ensure adherence to production schedules.

- Maintain effective liaison and communication with related departments in the company.

- Monitor and control operating costs so that they remain within the agreed level.

- Develop and recommend medium and long range plans for productivity improvement.

- Maintain effective communication with trade union officials and preserve good relations with them.

- Train and develop staff to meet agreed performance levels.

- Direct the preparation and presentation of revenue and cost budgets through liaison with senior managers.

- Observe all agreed working procedures and agreements aimed at maintaining effective industrial relations.

- Maintain product quality at the level agreed.

- Observe the statutory requirements affecting safety and conditions of service.

- Ensure that plant and equipment is maintained in a proper state of repair.

- Monitor and control sales by units and by revenue.

- Analyse costs so that any deviation can be effectively monitored and corrected.

- Prepare production schedules on monthly, weekly or daily basis.

- Plan, monitor and control work flow.

4. Checking Progress

How do you check how you're getting on?

- what information do you produce?
- who else is involved?
- who do you tell, and how (by reports, statistics, returns)?
- who else *needs* to know?
- do you have any regular meetings as part of this checking process?

You may find it helpful to combine key results and progress checks in a chart like this. (We've filled in a typical entry as an example of what each column should contain).

Job title:

KEY RESULT AREA	KEY RESULT	STANDARDS OF PERFORMANCE the conditions that exist if action is well done	CONTROL how is level of performance known?
Communication	Produce house magazine on almost nothing	4 editions per year	time, cost

5. Review Period

Some jobs involve change by their very nature. If this is the case it needs to be acknowledged, and one way of doing this is to agree on a review period. At the end of this period you can discuss your job description to check whether it still adequately describes what you do.

Does your job change, is it changing?
Is your organisation changing and if so, should your job be changing with it?

You may not know; if you're not sure then it might be a good idea to review your job description once a year just to find out – you may have a surprise! This would form an obvious part of your progress check about which there is more below.

If you know that your job is changing, then:

- what are the key changes?
- over what period are these changes happening?
- how often would it be useful to review your job: if it's too often, you may undermine your own confidence; if it's too infrequent that may allow your job description to become unrelated to the work and that can introduce uncertainty.

 WHAT ABOUT YOUR OWN JOB DESCRIPTION?

Now think about your own job description:

- if you already have one, look at it again to see if and how well it covers the points listed above

- if you don't, you'll find it well worthwhile writing one, bearing in mind the hints and examples we gave earlier.

REVIEWING YOUR PERFORMANCE

We've talked above about checking day-to-day achievement of goals. However, we also need to check how effectively we perform our job overall. Some firms do this through 'Job Reviews' or 'Performance Reviews' which necessarily involve other people. You can go through the basic process by yourself by listing a number of things about your work.

Here's a checklist you can use in a performance review:

● Have you an up-to-date and mutually agreed job description covering your position?

● Which key areas of the job have needed most of your attention in recent months?

- Thinking of the achievements in which you have played a direct part during the past year, which one or two gave you the most satisfaction?

- Which particular outcomes fell short of your expectation, if any?

- What main obstacles or difficulties have you had to overcome in recent months, if any?

- What problems or frustrations remain to be overcome in the future?

- Specify any areas of your job which you think could be developed.

- Specify any additional training, experience, information or resources that you need to maintain or improve your job performance.

- What are the main priorities in your action plan for the next few months?

- Specify any training or developments which you have undergone during the last year. What were the benefits, if any?

- What other matters do you feel could be usefully raised with your immediate manager during the review?

- When would you like to engage in a similar review of the situation?

Who Is Involved in a Review of Performance?

Discussions of your performance must involve you, but they must also involve your boss. Unless your boss, his boss and so on up the line have criteria for performance, it cannot be measured and so can't be really effective.

The discussion must be two-way but either you *or* your boss can initiate it (Of course, you may feel that you can't easily communicate with your boss. If that's the case we suggest you turn to page 70-73 for hints on how to cope with this problem.)

Others who may be interested in your performance include:

- those who are interested because it affects corporate interests (e.g. other people in the organisation, senior management)
- those who are interested because it has a ripple effect on their work (e.g. colleagues, staff)
- those who are interested because they are interested in you (e.g. personnel, family, friends, managers, colleagues)
- you.

Have You Met Your Objectives?

Now you have reached the end of this chapter check back to the list of objectives we gave at the beginning. Have you achieved all that you set out to?

 WHAT NEXT?
Your Agenda for Action

What else do you intend to do now?

● Can you develop your skills, knowledge or experience further? In what specific areas?

● Do you need a better written job description? If so, how will you go about obtaining one?

● Do you need to review any areas of your work, and in particular, any relating to your key results?

● Are you going to ask anybody to help you review your performance?

Elsewhere in the Book

This chapter has only started the process of looking at how you can work more effectively by providing a framework for looking at yourself and your job. In practice, there will be many other more specific factors or issues that will affect how you work and subsequent chapters are devoted to these. They will of course keep relating back to the issues that we have sketched above. Individual issues are dealt with in the book as follows:

Chapter 2 looks at time management.

Chapter 3 is about problem solving.

Chapter 4 is about your working environment.

Chapter 5 discusses working with other people.

Chapter 6 is about organising systems for storing things, so that you can find them again!

Chapter 7 is about change and how to handle it.

Chapter 8 is about coping with stress, switching off.

Help at Work

Do you have a job review system?
If so, are there any issues in this chapter which can be discussed during a job review?
If not, can one be set up?
Who could you ask?

2: THE RIGHT TASK AT THE RIGHT TIME

 After reading this chapter you will be able to:

- review how you use your time at present
- organise your use of time more effectively
- identify ways in which you can avoid wasting time
- achieve your time plans.

INTRODUCTION

The time we have available for work is limited. It should therefore be one of our top priorities to plan how much time to invest in any one job or task - but in practice it's the resource that many of us find hardest to organise.

The time we have available for work is limited.

We don't expect to be simply given extra cash, staff or premises every time we need more of them to do our jobs. We expect to put energy, time and planning into acquiring them. Yet we are often slipshod with our time – we don't plan it with care, and when we have it we don't always use it well.

There is no simple answer to the question 'how can we use time efficiently?'; to plan every minute of every day we would have to be machines. On the other hand, it is possible to budget time just as we budget other resources.

In this chapter, we identify three distinct stages in this process:

- LOOKING AT THE WAY IN WHICH YOU USE YOUR TIME AT PRESENT
- PLANNING YOUR TIME
- USING THE PLANNED TIME EFFECTIVELY.

HOW DO YOU USE YOUR TIME?

We suggest you start by recording how you already use your time; after all, unless you are about to leave your job, what you *already do* should offer some clues about what you *should be doing!*

A Time Log

A time log records how you spend your time, minute by minute through the day for a period of days. This method *may* suit your needs but:

- keeping a log itself takes a lot of time
- it makes you concentrate on detail rather than broad activity.

For this reason, it's probably best to keep a log only when you need to measure the exact time you use for particular purposes, such as how much time a week you spend travelling, how long you spend on the phone to different people or how much time you should allow for a particular operation or process.

One day I had to make five phone calls; I thought that I would make them before I did the main job I had planned for that morning. I finally finished them at 11.30 – too late to be able to get the main job of the morning finished. I need to plan my phoning much more precisely in future and to that end, I am keeping an exact log of phone calls for the next three weeks.

Keeping a Diary

Instead of a log, why not keep a diary? This records how you have used your time day by day rather than minute by minute; like any other diary, you can write it up in five minutes at the end of each day.

WRITE YOUR OWN DIARY

- Write a list of the things on which you have spent time, at the end of each day. Note everything you did.
- Take a typical period of activity – not a period when everyone's on holiday, when you are stocktaking or when your new computer is being installed!
- Make your list cover a span of at least two weeks.
- Include not just your time at work but time spent working - overtime, work at home, work done while travelling and so on.
- It might be useful to start with your job description, since this should bear some relation to what you do.
- Describe broad activities first rather than trivia.
- Make a note of how much time is spent on each. You might like to use a layout like this:

1. DAY & TIME SPENT	2. ACTIVITY	3. COMMENTS	4

- Column 3 is for you to write down any notes or thoughts that occur to you while completing the diary. We will also use it again later.

- Column 4 will be used shortly to see who decided that time should be used in this way.

Here is an example of one person's diary:

WHEN	WHAT	COMMENTS
TUESDAY		
8.30 – 3.30	Crewe: progress collaboration agreement with Browns	Browns: GM, TM & CM.
$2\frac{1}{2}$ hours	Draft revised agreement & letter to Browns G.M.	
WEDNESDAY		
8.30 – 9.30	Patents registrar, job definition – review	Patents man.
9.30 – 10.30	Patents officer annual appraisal	P.O. + P. Mgs
10.30 – 11.30	Patents registrar, job definition – review	P Mgs & Analyst
11.30 – 12.15	Review selection of office equipment	
1.30 – 2.30	Finalise Patents Officer appraisal	P. Mgs & Officer
30 mins.	Finalise letter to Browns & pass to secretary	Phone Browns contact.
30 mins	Review Tudor Park Project	Research officer
2 hours	Read morning mail & mark for attention.	

Who Decides How Your Time Should Be Used?

Once you have filled in your diary you need to know how much control you in fact have over your use of time at work. Your time could be controlled in a number of ways:

- you might control it totally yourself

- your boss might have a lot of say over how much time you spend doing what and when

- if you work regularly as part of a group or team, the group may itself create a pressure for time to be used in a particular way

- the organisation you work for may lay down rules

- the system or industry you work in may control your time – for example if you are responsible for recruitment, you may have a number of people to interview but you may not be in a position to influence precisely how many and when.

 EXPLORE YOUR TIME CONTROL

Compare the way you actually used your time with how you had planned to use it (by comparing the diary above with your appointments diary perhaps).

In the diary above, use column 4 for 'Time Control'. Against each item, make a note of two things:

- who controlled that aspect of your time?

- can it be changed or is it absolutely fixed?

Now that you have prepared a diary you have a baseline from which to start time planning.

TIME PLANNING

Planning often means no more than starting the week with a vague intention to do certain jobs, taking on extra commitments as they arise, ending the week with a number of things that haven't been done (things of varying importance) which may or may not get carried forward to the next week. To avoid this situation, we need to predict the things that are likely to influence our use of time . If we do this well, we will be half way to *achieving* our targets.

Things to consider include:

● Time periods

● Targets

● Priorities

● Time allocation

● The right time.

Time Periods

How much time should you use for planning-days, weeks, months, something else? It will depend very much on the type of work you do.

Targets

What are you hoping to achieve in a given period, i.e. what are your *targets*?

Priorities

Decide priorities by *need* not preference; for example:

• what is the relative urgency of different tasks?
• what targets and deadlines do you *have* to meet?
• what happens if you don't achieve certain deadlines or targets?
• what effect does a particular task have on other people's work?
• which tasks are essential, which incidental?

(You may like to use your key areas from the previous chapter as check for how 'essential' a task is.)

You can label your tasks as

- **Musts:** it is essential to do them
- **Needs:** it is preferable to do them
- **Wants:** it would be nice to do them

The Unfinished Job

If tasks don't get done – does that matter?

If it does matter then you should ask:

- are your priorities wrong?
- have you got too much to do? If so, lose some or share some!
- can you do some jobs in less time – is there any room for time saving by delegation, getting help, or automation?

If some things don't get done but it doesn't much matter, you may still have to do something about those things:

- can you throw them away?
- should you tell someone?
- can you pass them on?

Remember, even if some jobs are not done, you will have been successful in your goals if you have finished your key jobs

TIME ALLOCATION

How much time should you allow for each activity? This includes not only the time needed to perform a task but also the other things you have to do, so that the task can be performed. These may include travel, filing, writing, phoning, handling things that go wrong, niceties (being polite to people may take time but may be essential to your successful completion of a job). You must allow time for development and improvement – do you do this? (Working through this book should be taking place during such a time!)

Make sure your estimates are *realistic* – one of the biggest causes of bad time management is unrealistic targets in the first place.

The Right Time

When is the right time for you? We all have a personal time clock that varies daily, weekly and monthly. For example:

- do you work better early or late in the day?
- do you work better before or after meals?
- which days of the week are most effective for you – and least effective?
- are there times in the month when you work less efficiently?
- is your work ever affected by external factors, for example the side effects of travel?

If your performance does fluctuate build this into your time plan. For example:

- are there jobs which you *know* will be difficult? If so can they be done at the times when you perform best?
- can less important and routine things be collected for times of less effective performance?

NOW WRITE YOUR OWN TIME PLAN

Use this space to make notes for your own time plan.

Time period for this plan:

1.*	2. LIST OF TASKS	3. INCIDENTALS (e.g. travel)	4. TIME ALLOWED

*Now put the tasks in column 2 in priority order by writing 'a', 'b' or 'c' in column 1.

'a' means that this job is a must.
'b' means that this job is a need.
'c' means that this job is only a want.

If you want to carry this a stage further, for example, if you have a very large number of jobs to sort out, you can add i, ii, iii, etc to all those labelled 'a' and so on, to get a complete list.

●   Can you achieve all the tasks in the time allowed? What will you do with the ones you can't achieve?

YOUR PERSONAL TIME CLOCK

This chart is designed to help you decide which tasks to do when.

	early am	mid am	noon	mid pm	late pm	evening
Monday						
Tuesday						
Wednesday						
Thursday						
Friday						
Saturday *						
Sunday *						

*   if you work at weekends

- Shade in (a) the periods when you work best
    - (b) the periods when you work at average pace
    - (c) the periods when you don't work very well.

Use highlighter pens, with a different colour for each type of period. If you don't have highlighters, just note (a), (b), (c) in a corner of each box.

- Do change the headings at the top of the columns if your work is differently organised (if for instance you work mainly at night).

- Now add the main tasks from the previous activity on to this chart, putting the most urgent tasks in the times of high effectiveness, the routine jobs in the average periods and using the periods of low effectiveness for rest breaks or very undemanding jobs.

ACHIEVING YOUR TARGETS

This means achieving the right thing *on time*.
Remember, **next week isn't there** – what's planned for this week must be done this week.

You can only achieve your targets if:

- Your plan has been properly worked out in the first place.

- You avoid diversions and distractions – we discuss these below.

- You take positive steps to achieve the things you've got to do - these are also discussed below.

DIVERSIONS AND DISTRACTIONS

Task Avoidance

Are there any items in your diary you could mark with an 'A' in column 3 to note that you have been trying to avoid them? If there are, it could be because

- you *can't do* the task

- you have *difficulty getting started*

- you find the task *difficult*.

Can't Do It

If you can't do a job, you should ask yourself whether it should be passed to someone else to do; alternatively, you could find out how to do it! You may like to check first, though, that it's not just a question of getting started.

Can't Get Started

If you have difficulty getting started, you could try out some ways to help you get going. For example:

- creating an artificial source of pressure on yourself such as asking someone to check in half an hour that you have got started using a more straightforward, warm-up job

- getting someone to talk the job through with you

- allowing yourself a 'treat' (e.g. a cup of coffee, or a cigarette if you smoke) only after you have got started

- if the job involves writing, start writing – the mere action of writing can get your brain working.

Too Difficult

If a task *is* too difficult, get help. Ask someone, look up a book or other reference source. Asking for help isn't a sign of weakness; it's a useful skill that can be developed just like any other.

 # WHAT DO YOU AVOID DOING?

Make a list of things you avoid doing.

For each item, note why you avoid it – is it because you can't do it, you can't get started, or because you need help?

Just acknowledging that you do avoid certain things is often a help in dealing with them.

What else might you do about each of these items?

Genuine Diversions

These will happen in any job.

● Be ready to say 'No' to somebody's request if it is less important than what you have to do.

● If you do respond, remember that adding an extra job to your list means something else must be dropped – which will it be?

● If a diversion is unavoidable, perhaps part of your job, then allow specific times of the day for dealing with it.

POSITIVE AIDS

Improving our use of time isn't just a question of avoiding negative influences. There are positive steps we can take. These include

● delegating

● using meetings properly

● the creative use of diaries

● pacing ourselves.

Let's look at each of these in turn:

Delegating

Staff get frustrated if their own boss does not delegate to them. Do you:

● carry out tasks (specially routine ones) that others could do for you?

● have access to people to carry out those tasks?
  If so, do delegate!

People can take on a surprising amount of responsibility and often work better as a result. It is better to have an empty desk top, time to talk to other staff and time to think than to have so many things to do that you can't think about organising them better, can't take time to brief other people to do them, can't find time in the end to do the jobs themselves. The most productive people are often the ones who can take on more work - that is because they *delegate*.

WHAT BENEFITS WOULD YOU GAIN BY DELEGATING MORE?

Spend five minutes noting down ways in which you could delegate more. Use the three columns below for your notes, and make a decision to put your ideas into effect at the next opportunity.

What will I delegate?	Who will I delegate to?	How will this delegation benefit me?

There is a longer discussion about how to delegate in Chapter 5, *Working with People*.

Telephone Tips

We spend a lot of time using the phone yet we don't always use it well. Using it efficiently can save money as well as time. Some points to consider are:

● Can you use a telephone answering machine? Is there someone who can take telephone messages for you? When you don't want to be disturbed can you reroute calls?

● Could you make all your calls at one time (e.g. mid-afternoon, when calls are cheaper)?

● Could you arrange to have a private line so that you can make urgent outgoing calls even if the incoming line is busy or connected to the machine?

● If you have a system for intercepting your calls, do call back when you have time, otherwise you will rapidly lose credibility.

Meeting Tips

We spend a lot of time in meetings. These are discussed in more depth in Chapter 5, *Working with People*, but there are a few points about meetings to be made here:

● If the meetings are regularly a waste of time, cancel them or make sure their purpose or conduct is changed.

● If you can avoid going yourself, delegate attendance to someone else.

● Make sure they're punctual – be there on time, make sure other people are, agree on a time for ending them and stick to it.

● Make sure they are properly chaired – do it yourself or try to ensure that someone efficient does so.

● Do your homework.

● Hold them in other people's offices so that you can leave when you want to.

Diary Tips

When using your diary:

● Treat key jobs as 'appointments with yourself' and give them a diary slot - keep interruption-free times on a regular basis for this purpose if necessary.

● Use your diary to set yourself deadlines.

● Group together activities such as telephoning, correspondence, reading, talking to staff and colleagues, resting, and allocate time for them.

● If you're making appointments, arrange for one to follow another so that each one *has* to end by a specified time.

● Have only one key diary, don't have several in different places with different people making appointments for you. You might like to think about who can see it – it's helpful for colleagues to know that you have times committed to particular things.

Other Tips

There are many other tips which we can offer and which you can collect for yourself. For example:

- Only handle papers once.

- Never put off a difficult task – it will only get more difficult to tackle.

- Add handwritten answers to the original and then copy it.

- Read selectively.

- Manage by exception, i.e. don't look at all the routine information but only at things that are out of the ordinary.

- Work at home only if it helps both home and work.

- Don't have an open door policy – make sure everyone knows when you are available and when you must not be disturbed.

- Use labour-saving devices. Word-processors, computers and calculators are obvious job-aids but don't forget simple things such as rubber stamps and guillotines.

Pacing Yourself

We deal with this in more detail in Chapter 8, *Switching Off*. However, there are some immediate rules about pacing yourself that affect time management:

- Try to plan the next day at the end of each day and the next week at the end of each week.

- Make sure you have breaks between each large job.

- Don't work on a very concentrated task for too long without a break – for example, meetings, working at a VDU, driving.

- Try and complete a job completely before going on to the next one – don't leave odd bits and pieces to be done before you can get started on the next job. When finishing a meeting, make sure any action points have been fed into your system to be brought forward.

WHICH TIPS WILL YOU USE?

Make a note *now* of any of the above tips you think would be helpful.

Add any more you can think of yourself.

Is there anyone you can share these tips with?

Do you have colleagues who could contribute their own tips?

 ## Have You Met Your Objectives?

Now that you have worked through this chapter check back to the list of objectives that we gave at the start. Have you achieved all you set out to?

WHAT NEXT?

 ## Your Agenda for Action

What else do you intend to do now?

● Do you need to work on any ways of using time in more detail?

● Do you need to explore further any of the issues we've discussed?

● Are you confident that you will use your time well in the next year?

Having worked through this chapter and tried some of the ideas, you might like to write another diary and compare it with the one you wrote at the beginning of the chapter.

Elsewhere in the Book

You will find useful tips in some other chapters about issues which also have an effect on time management:

Chapter 3 offers approaches to handling problems and difficulties.

Chapter 4 looks at your place of work and highlights factors which may affect your work.

Chapter 5 is about working with people and so has more about communications and meetings.

Chapter 6 is about information storage and retrieval and should provide ideas about having the right document at the right time.

Chapter 7 is about change, which affects long-term time planning.

Chapter 8 is about stress and lists ideas which should help in pacing yourself.

Help at Work

What sources of help with time management are there available to you at work?

● Does your training department run any courses?

● Do you have any managers who can help implement a development programme?

● Is there any way you can get together with colleagues to share ideas about managing time?

3: WHEN THE GOING GETS TOUGH

 After reading this chapter you will be able to:

- predict routine problems in your work
- cope with unexpected problems
- handle problems effectively.

INTRODUCTION

However well we plan, problems do occur. They must be resolved; otherwise they may grow out of proportion and affect everything else, make our time planning ineffective, divert us from our objectives, cause stress.

Here are examples of some of the problems facing an engineer working in systems engineering:

My boss wants a preview of next Monday's presentation at 8.30 am tomorrow; some foils aren't yet prepared or typed – to attend his meeting will require two meetings to be postponed tomorrow morning. I'll probably have to work through lunch and get the stuff typed this afternoon.

I can't find the papers for the meeting at 11.00.

The recruitment is behind schedule and making little progress.

The department's objectives are not sufficiently well understood to carry out staff appraisal effectively; staff appraisal is extremely complex and difficult to handle in a situation when staff are primarily working in taskforces on customers' sites with only occasional contact and supervision from the department.

Each of these problems could be solved simply by taking the right approach. That means reacting in a systematic way and not panicking or bodging.

In this chapter we'll be looking at ways of dealing effectively with problems in general. We will not be looking at ways of tackling specific problems but we will aim to develop some basic guidelines for you to apply to your own work.

WHAT SORT OF PROBLEM?

A problem is an obstacle to progress; it need not necessarily be big nor even harmful – it is only a problem because of its side effects.

 WHAT PROBLEMS ARE YOU FACED WITH AT WORK?

Make a list of unresolved problems that you currently have to deal with at work.
They may be large or small.
They may not all cause you anxiety – in fact many of them probably do not.

A problem is an obstacle to progress.

Managing director requires slight shift of emphasis on department's objectives without the opportunity to change budjets to reflect this

Secondment of overseas visitor into customers taskforce not running smoothly

In-tray virtually unattended for four days

Difficulties of establishing a satisfactory and effective means of coding, storing and retrieving documents greater than perceived – will need to allocate some resources to solve the problem and seek further advice

Serious bottlenect apparent in taskforce launch tracking over the next four months – will have an impact on start dates and in turn on our financial results

An important feature of the above list – and we hope this is also true of your own - is that the problems listed are not all of the same magnitude. In particular, some are routine and some are crises. This distinction can be a very useful one.

Routine or Crisis?

First, a quick summary of the routine/crisis distinction:

- a ROUTINE problem is a regular feature of our work

- a CRISIS is a problem that is unforeseen or irregular.

Routine Problems are problems that you can predict and plan for. For example, a machine that is in regular use can be expected to break down; that is minimised by regular servicing. Since it will still break down occasionally, there will probably be someone on hand whose job it is to make repairs.

Crises are problems which arise unexpectedly. For example, a freak thunder storm may flood your office and soak the carpets. No one can avoid crises altogether but those that do occur should do so because they are *unavoidable*. For example, the cost of replacing the carpets will probably be less than the cost of putting in storm drains just in case of an infrequent flood.

 ROUTINE OR CRISIS?

Are the items in your list of unresolved problems routine or crises? Relist them here under the respective heading:

Routine Problems	*Crises*

Once you have identified these two main types of problem, you can begin to work out ways of dealing with them.

● If they are *routine* problems, they can be predicted and so we can plan for them.

● If they are *crises*, we can still minimise their effects by devising ways of handling them.

48

PLANNING FOR PROBLEMS

Planning for problems involves:

● Planning the work itself
● Training staff and preparing them to handle problems
● Having contingency plans for handling problems that do arise

Work Planning

Basic ways of avoiding problems in general include:

● setting objectives
● breaking jobs into manageable tasks.

Objectives

Setting objectives for a job or task focusses our attention on the essential job, helps us avoid being side-tracked. This helps us avoid problems because:

● identifying the essential job means we can carry it out more effectively
● objectives should be measurable and achievable. If we fail to achieve them we can check performance and pinpoint exactly where the problem occurred.

 ## SETTING OBJECTIVES

Which of these two jobs do you think is least likely to go wrong? Put a circle round the instruction that is most likely to get the required results.

'See to Mr Smith's car. It needs a service and checking out and it's not firing properly and while you're about it, he's not too happy with the way it's going, and it's the 25,000 mile service.'

'Mr Smith's Car:

● do a 25,000 mile service
● check the plugs
● check the carburettor
● test to see that it is running properly.'

We hope you picked the second instruction. Why? Because it's the clearest. It sets down the precise activities that the mechanic should carry out; it gives specific objectives rather than vague pointers to what needs to be done.

Breaking Jobs Into Manageable Tasks

Once you have set objectives you should:

- analyse the job into separate tasks
- allocate enough time for each task
- sort the tasks into the right order
- identify points where you should make checks or where extra inputs might be needed because of potential problems.

Staff Training

If you employ others don't forget that they need training to build up their problem-handling skills.

 DEVELOPING PROBLEM-HANDLING SKILLS

Look back to your list of problems on p. 46. For each one, note down:

- what skills you need to develop to handle the problem better
- how your staff or colleagues would benefit from having these skills too.

In Chapter 1, we invited you to list possible areas of self-development – you might like to refer back to this section. Skills that you might develop to improve problem-solving are:

- developing self-confidence and self-awareness
- developing specific technical skills.

SELF CONFIDENCE AND AWARENESS

Self confidence can be developed by:

   identifying strengths, and then building on them

   understanding areas of weakness, and then working on them (this might include how to handle anxieties).

Many types of training provide this type of personal development – in-company, through professional bodies, through the educational system and through self-help groups.

Self-monitoring and skills in handling situations can also be fostered by self-help arrangements at work (e.g. the use of quality circles).

TECHNICAL SKILLS

Any technical processes will cover much to do with breakdowns and problems.

In addition courses and training are widely available in:

* health and safety

   first aid

   fire control

If you are employed by a company or organisation some training will almost certainly be available at your place of work.

SOLVING PROBLEMS ONCE THEY HAVE OCCURRED

If a problem *does* occur despite your planning, take steps to solve it promptly.

   analyse and describe it if possible – problems are more easily solved when they have been written down or shared with someone else

* don't leave an unsolved problem undealt with or worse, half dealt with; if everyone else thinks you are dealing with a problem they will probably leave you to get on with it – but if in fact you're not, what will happen then?

Let's look at this in more detail.

ANALYSE YOUR OWN PROBLEM

At the beginning of the chapter, we invited you to note some problems that you currently have to handle. Use this checklist to analyse one of the problems on your list. If you find it helpful, keep a copy of the list handy and use it to tackle fresh problems – some are bound to occur before long!

The problem:

1. What is the situation that is causing concern?

2. Who is responsible for it?

3. What caused it?

4. Who can help with it?

5. What steps can be taken to deal with it?

6. Who is going to carry out these steps?

7. How will you know whether the remedy has worked?

8. Who will check the outcome?

The Unresolved Problem

What about problems that can't be solved? Here are some hints on how to cope when all other approaches have failed.

Ask yourself:

- Have I stated the problem correctly? (Don't confuse cause and effect).

- Is the problem *my* problem at all?

- Should I pass the problem on to someone else who *can* deal with it?

In the end, if you do leave a problem unresolved check this with your manager or a colleague. Make sure that they know what you are doing and agree with your decision.

Going it alone

One group of problems we haven't tackled so far are those that arise because of isolation. The solitary worker has to cope with these problems without the benefit of a boss or colleague to talk to. Typical issues that face people working on their own are:

- difficulty in keeping attention focussed, staying interested in the work

- lack of clear goals to work towards

- absence of any way of appraising performance.

Attention and Interest

If you find it hard to concentrate your attention on the work in hand, check:

- Have you removed irrelevant and unwanted stimuli, e.g. noise, hunger, cold?

- Have you put aside other pressing, non-work matters? You could deal with these by simply listing them as 'to-dos' and allocating a set time for them after your working hours.

- Can you cultivate further interest in your work? Perhaps you are doing something that is part of a larger system or process. Why not spend some time finding out more about the wider context of your work?

Goals

We discussed targets and objectives in some detail in Chapter 1. If you are a solitary worker these will be particularly important – and you'll need to generate them *yourself*. Some ways of providing and using clearly defined goals include:

- Having clear, realistic goals for every work session: you might find it helpful to jot these down and tick them off as you achieve them

- Developing an awareness of what motivates you and keeping clearly in mind the connection between it and the work in hand.

Self-appraisal

Set aside clear periods for appraising your progress. This applies to any job, but it becomes even more vital if you work alone. A good rule of thumb might be half an hour at the end of each week and a good half-day in every month.

Have You Met Your Objectives?

Now that you have completed this chapter check back to the list of objectives we gave at the beginning. Have you achieved all those you set out to achieve?

WHAT NEXT?

 Your Agenda for Action

What else do you intend to do now?

● Do you have any unresolved problems that you would now like to get rid of?

● Are there any skills you need to acquire to improve your performance in this area?

● Can you get together with colleagues to plan joint approaches to problem avoidance and problem solving?

Elsewhere in the Book

Chapter 1 covers your objectives and key areas so is relevant to predicting problem areas.

Chapter 2 is about time management and will be relevant if there are problems associated with timing.

Chapter 4 is about your place of work and should highlight areas there which might cause problems.

Chapter 5 is about working with people, working well with them so as to avoid problems.

Chapter 6 is about finding things easily when you want them, so as to avoid the problem of losing them!

Chapter 7 is about change, predicting and handling it without it causing problems.

Chapter 8 is about stress, avoiding it and the problems associated with it.

54

Help at Work

Where can you find relevant training in your company?

- training department?
- at appraisal interviews – with your boss?
- through the personnel department?
- through the open learning unit?

 You may like to make a note of relevant training opportunities your company offers:

4: YOU AND YOUR WORKPLACE

 After reading this chapter you will be able to:

- identify the factors in your working environment which can affect efficient working
- suggest beneficial changes that could be made in your own environment
- get such changes made.

INTRODUCTION

Almost everyone who works – even people who work at home – reserves a space which is their working area, whether it is a workshop, an office, a room or just a table. Indeed those who don't very quickly discover that they are attempting the impossible!

Whether it is a small work area or a large industrial site, the place and space in which we work has a great impact on how effective we are. In this chapter we'll look at ways in which we can ensure our workplace helps, and doesn't hinder effective working.

To start with, the type of work may itself impose certain constraints and conditions - for example the layout of equipment, side products of processes and so on.

These may be controlled by Health and Safety regulations and by a variety of other national or local authority laws and company rules.

There may also be influences that we can't identify because we don't fully understand them; new materials or processes are often developed faster than our understanding of their side effects. For example, we learned to use asbestos years before we understood its hazard to health.

In thinking about our working environment there are two issues to tackle:

- WHAT THINGS HAVE AN IMPACT ON US?

- HOW MUCH CONTROL DO WE HAVE?

Here is a typical toolroom in a large factory.
Nearly everything is fixed – there is very little scope for short-term changes.

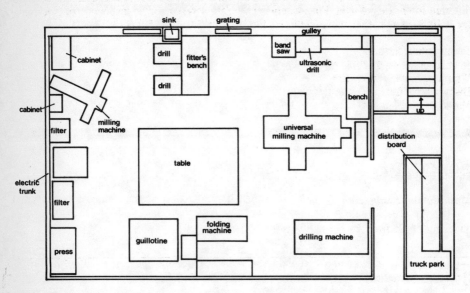

WHAT THINGS HAVE AN IMPACT ON YOU?

Environment

This includes:

- heating or cooling, temperature, etc
- ventilation, fresh air, etc
- dust and fumes
- lighting
- equipment, its by products, and the side effects of working with it for long periods.

Here are some basic environmental guidelines. The list is not intended to be exhaustive, but it does cover some of the key influences in any working environment:

Optimum temperature (°F)

Light sedentary work: winter 68 – 73
Light sedentary work: summer 75 – 80
Moderate hard work : 65
Strenuous work : 60

58

Lighting

Specific guidelines are difficult to give. However, it's worth bearing in mind that different activities need different intensities of light. For example, if we rate a very detailed inspection of electronics circuitry at 100% illumination, minimum levels for other tasks rate as follows:

Proofreading: 30%
Regular office work: 20%
Wrapping and labelling: 10%
Dishwashing: 6%
Materials handling: 4%

Maximum safe noise level

About 80-90 decibels
(equivalent to sitting inside a bus in city traffic).

Typical ventilation requirement

30-40 cubic metres of fresh air per person.

 THE TRAINING ROOM

'We had to run this course in a factory – it was on health and safety! A training room with a false ceiling had been built in one corner of the factory. It was so well built that there was no ventilation, but the walls were so thin it was very cold. So they brought in a gas heater. Well, that gave off fumes and because of the lack of ventilation the atmosphere became very dubious. Even though I was helping to run the course, I kept nodding off!'

Layout

Efficient use of space is crucial if we are to reach things easily without also creating hazards. If you work in an enclosed area you should have at least 4 square metres of space to yourself – including space taken up by furniture. If you work sitting down your work surface should be about 71-76cm high (for writing) or 66-71cm high (for typing). Here are four further hints on how to achieve effective layout:

- try to ensure that routine journeys are:
  short
  straight
  on one level

- lay out your workspace so that items you need to glance at frequently (e.g. charts, dials, colleagues) lie directly ahead of you.

- if your work entails frequent reaching for things (e.g. books or tools) make sure those items you need most often are within easiest reach.

- if you often have to use two pieces of equipment at once (e.g. answer the phone and write down a message) make sure you can easily reach both items simultaneously.

Make sure you can reach both items simultaneously.

 WHAT'S YOUR WORKSPACE LIKE?

Are these features of your workplace satisfactory? Refer back to the guidelines on the previous page if necessary.

	Yes	No	Comments
Temperature			
Ventilation			
Dust/fume extraction			
Side effects of equipment			

Are there any items of equipment which influence the way you use your workspace?

Are there any materials you work with that impose special constraints on how you work?

For any problems you have identified:

- select those that you have
- make a note *now* of what action you can take to remedy them. Set yourself a clear deadline for this.

What Sort of Environment Suits You Personally?

In addition to the factors that affect everyone, there are things that can help or hinder your individual performance. For example:

- Your personal needs (whether you are short or tall, have good or poor eyesight and hearing, suffer from any allergies, suffer from back problems and so on).

- Your personal preferences (are you a 'mole' or a 'kangaroo' – do you like to hide away in a corner or hop around the office?).

- The needs of your own work situation (do you need a drawing board, a typewriter, a computer, a telephone, all of these?).

 # WHAT ABOUT YOUR WORKSPACE?

Draw a rough sketch of your workspace – it may be a desk top, an office, a workshop.

Put a red ring around the things you would like to or should change.

Compare your results with the two examples below. The first shows a complete office. Commenting on the plan the person who drew it said:

'The thing I find most frustrating about this office is the placing of power points. The microcomputer has most leads and so gets a point to itself. But our secretary needs a lead for her typewriter and this has to trail across to the same point. Then there's the placing of my own desk in the bay-window, which is too cold in winter and too warm in summer. Finally, the filing cabinets are placed too far from our secretary's desk: if we could put in an extra point on their side of the room the cabinets could be swapped with the micro and Dianne wouldn't have to cross the path of people entering the room to read them'.

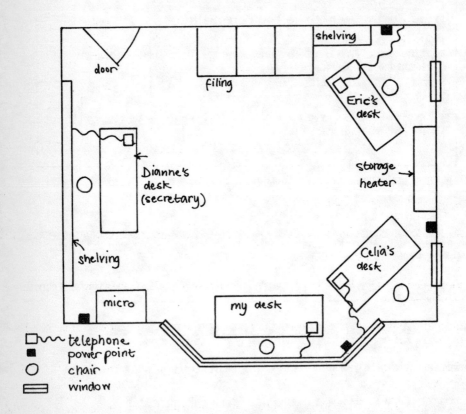

Do you agree with this diagnosis? Is it the only solution? What about the cold bay-window?

The second example shows a desk top from the same office.

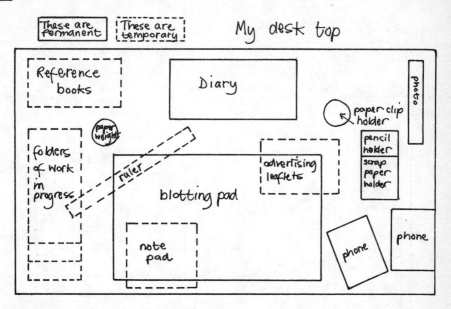

 What would you want to change if this was your desk top?
Think about it for a few moments, then read on.

Some of the points noted by the owner of the desk were:

- the paper-clip holder isn't really necessary – I hardly ever use it, and have a trayful of clips in one of my desk drawers

- the folders of work in progress could be set out next to each other for ease of access. Their position could be taken up by my diary instead.

- the paperweight and the tray are unnecessary: I like to personalise my desk-top but the photo is enough for that.

- I shouldn't really have two phones: but I've kept putting off a request for a more sophisticated model that registers incoming calls while I'm talking on an outside line.

SAFETY AT WORK

Safety at work may not be one of the most exciting of topics but it's undoubtedly one of the keys to effective working. Just consider: every year over 5000 injuries are sustained by office staff – and these are only the injuries that keep people off work for three days or more!

Use the following checklist to rate your own workspace for safety. If you answer No to any points insert a further tick to remind yourself *either* to take action yourself or, where appropriate to tell someone else. If you work in a business of any size one member of staff is likely to have overall responsibility for ensuring your workplace is safe.

SAFETY CHECKLIST

Tick:	Yes	No	Can you rectify?	Who should you tell?
Are any of the floor or stair surfaces slippery?				
Are any of the stair or floor coverings worn or badly tacked down?				
Are any handrails damaged or missing?				
Are any corridors or alleyways obstructed by furniture or parcels?				
Are any telephone or electrical leads left trailing?				
Are filing cabinet drawers left open?				
Is furniture comfortable and well-designed?				
Is your workspace clean?				
Are your cloakroom facilities adequate?				
Are light-switches well-placed?				
Do you, or anyone else, have to lift, carry or move a load so heavy as to be a likely cause of injury?				

HOW MUCH CONTROL DO YOU HAVE?

It's not a lot of help to think about your working environment if you can't change it. That's dependent on how much control we can exercise over it which in turn may be affected by:

● Organisational constraints, e.g. the layout of a production line, work flow, needs of the machinery, where materials or information are stored.

● Management decisions about organisational needs and use of space.

● Colleagues – in an office, that may be *all* the people sharing the office.

● Yourself. Your work space may just be a desk top or a whole workshop or office – can you carry out changes in it?

 YOUR CHECKLIST

On the sketch of your workspace, put a green ring around the things you can change yourself.

Things that are circled with both red and green suggest immediate action.
Using that sketch and the checklist of environmental factors make a list of things to do to improve your working environment.

Things to change	Who do you need to talk to about it?	Action?

Have You Met Your Objectives?

Now that you have worked through this chapter check back to the list of objectives that we gave at the beginning. Have you achieved all that you set out to?

WHAT NEXT?

 Your Agenda for Action

What else do you intend to do now?

- In what areas could you or should you take action?

- Can you start to improve things in your own area, including measures for cost reduction or improved efficiency?

- How should you do this, who should you discuss it with?

Elsewhere in the Book

Chapter 3 is about problem solving – if you find it difficult to achieve some desired changes, that could be a problem.

Chapter 5 is about working with other people; part of that involves sharing space.

Chapter 6 is about organising information and other things needed in your job - that has implications for space use.

Chapter 7 is about change; changes may have an immediate impact on space organisation and use.

Chapter 8 is about switching off – it's important to have separate spaces for working and for the rest of your life if you are to switch off totally.

Help at Work

Where can you find relevant help in your company?

Is there a health and safety representative who can give you advice and help?

Can your boss help?

5: WORKING WITH PEOPLE

 After reading this chapter you will be able to:

- demonstrate what makes a team work
- delegate more effectively
- identify which of your communication skills you would like to improve.

INTRODUCTION

Other people can be one of our biggest aids to effective working. Yet many things that involve people are also among the most frustrating. How many meetings end up making you angry? How often do you get frustrated in your work because of things *other people* do or don't do?

Things other people do ...

We deal with people in a variety of settings:

- as individuals, perhaps boss and staff, supplier and customer
- in a small group, such as a team, the people in the same office
- in a large group, for example a department
- in a very large impersonal group, such as an organisation or large company.

But let's look, not just at the numbers of people we are involved with at a time but also at *how* we are involved with them. We contact people in three different ways in the course of our work:

● INFORMAL CONTACTS, for example asking a colleague to comment on a report you've written before it's circulated, chatting with people in the canteen; these contacts may not affect your work directly.

● LINE MANAGEMENT, for example delegating a task to someone; this is a more formal process though there is also direct contact between the two people involved.

● TASK GROUPS, a team of three or four people set up to complete a task; these may be short or long term.

These groups are all within an organisation but the same principles apply to contacts made by people working on their own. Let's see how far your own contacts can be classified in this way.

 ## WHAT PEOPLE DO YOU WORK WITH?

Make a list of the people you see in a week (if that's too many make it a day).

Are they:

- formal contacts
- line management
- task groups
- other?

We will use this information again later.

ONE PERSON'S CONTACTS DURING A WEEK

The management team from the electronics division of a company I work with
Patents manager
Patents officer
Job evaluation analyst
Secretary
Research scientist in the semiconductors department
Research director
Director of product technology
Manager, products division
Works engineer
Commercial controller
General manager, a sister company
Financial administrator
Lawyer, central legal department
Technical assessment manager
Section leader, semiconductors department

The most striking feature of this list is the sheer *variety* of people concerned; a general manager and a research director on the one hand, a secretary and a section leader on the other. For each of these people you'll need to adopt a specific style of communicating. However, there is one basic principle which underlies good working relationships: to respect them, whoever they are. This involves:

respecting their privacy
respecting confidences
being direct – look people in the eye when talking to them
not criticising them in public
repaying debts, favours and compliments, however small
standing up for them in their absence.

STAFF AND THEIR BOSS

What do employees expect of their boss? Managers have a big impact on the effectiveness of the people they manage. Here is some advice from one group of employees:

Have a good fix on your objectives; this provides staff with a sense of direction.

Have a well-developed plan for reaching your objectives; this gives staff the feeling that they are carrying out a sound programme.

● Keep staff informed of progress; this gives them a sense of participation.

● Treat staff as individuals; a leader can motivate a group only when he/she has learned how to motivate each person in the group.

● Accept nothing less than their best effort; they want to respect you and they cannot respect a leader who is satisfied with indifferent standards of accomplishment.

● Recognise their superior achievement; this demonstrates your impartiality and fairness.

● Follow up things that have been started.

● Lead. They know that is your job.

Getting on with your boss

We've just looked at some hints for being an effective manager. But what can you do, in the short term, when your own manager proves *ineffective?* In the table below we give some typical managerial shortcomings and possible ways in which you, as a subordinate, might get round them. Do bear in mind though, that the solutions are

●	short-term	– there's no substitute for effective managerial training that ensures problems *don't* occur.
●	last resorts	– in most cases we assume that you would try the solutions only when other avenues (for example honest discussion) have failed.

How to cope with your boss

Is your boss . . .   *If so, could you . . .*

Hard to get hold of?
- Find alternative ways of getting answers/information?

- Pass on the problem?

- Use his/her secretary to find out exactly when they are free?

70

Indecisive?	– Ask questions that set out clear alternatives?
	– Make clear the need for a decision when this is pressing?
	– Take more decisions yourself, where this is in your brief?
Sexist?	– Explain to him/her as tactfully as possible your reaction to/feelings about his/her behaviour?
	– Be sexist back, to make your point?
Vague, when making requests?	– Ask for clarification at the time?
	– Agree on a clear list of points you need to know about in order to carry out routine tasks effectively?
	– Give your boss a clear idea of what is involved in carrying out any specific instruction?
Forgetful, untidy or disorganised?	– Design systems that will function independent of him/her?
	– Discuss the matter with your/his/her secretary?
	– Make sure you retain records and duplicate copies of anything passed to them?
Liable to hold priorities and values that differ from your own (e.g. by seeing speed as more important than quality)?	– Adapt, but reserve some space in your job where you can operate in a way that satisfies *you?*
	– Find out what your ultimate customers want: this may change your mind *or* that of your boss?

Inconsistent?	– Tactfully remind him/her of past policies/decisions?
	– Ask for policies/decisions in writing?
	– Find out why – the reason may be inconsistency elsewhere in your organisation which you *both* find frustrating?
Unwilling to make positive comments about your performance	– Elicit these comments by tactful questioning?
	– Find someone else to comment on your work?
Unwilling to give negative comments on your performance?	– Explain your need to him/her?
	– Propose a regular, honest review of your work?
	– Find someone else willing to help review your work?
Unrealistic in what he/she demands (e.g. by exceeding your job description or available time)?	– Ask for a review/update of your job description?
	– Draw up your own schedule of tasks and ensure your boss knows about it?
	– Review the way you carry out tasks: are you being *too* exacting? Could you delegate more?
Uncommunicative about meetings arranged, decisions made?	– Ask more questions?
	– Ask to be included when memos and minutes are circulated?
	– Decide *why* you need a particular item of information and make sure your boss knows why?

Unwilling to talk about pressing problems (e.g. financial)?	– Find out why (you may be describing the problem in a threatening way)?
	– Agree on a set time to discuss a particular problem, and stick to it?
	– Pass on the problem?
	– Break down one big problem into several smaller, less daunting ones and ask to discuss each in turn?
Slow to respond to requests (e.g. for guidance or clarification)?	– Make a point of explaining why speed of reply is important?
	– Note down in your diary times to remind him/her (though beware of overdoing this!)?
	– Agree on a joint approach with your colleagues – a repeated request may be more effective if made by several people?
	– Put your request in writing?
	– Make it easy for him/her to say 'yes'?

Delegation

We mentioned delegation in Chapter 2 as one way of making good use of time. Here are some basic hints on good delegation:

Who Can You Delegate To?

Who are the people *you* can delegate to? They may not all be people you are responsible for. You may like to note down names but it may be more helpful to note job titles – people do change but the job will possibly still be there.

What Can You Delegate?

Are there jobs which *should* be done by somebody else (in other words their responsibility)? Are there jobs which *could* be done by somebody else?

How Do You Delegate?

If you delegate at random that won't be satisfactory for the other person; it's better to do it systematically by a regular daily or weekly briefing, an agreed paper-flow system and so on. If you have agreed to delegate, make sure that you pass all relevant material to the person concerned – to delegate and then not follow it through is the cause of much bad feeling, as well as being inefficient.

How Do They Feed Back?

Don't look over their shoulder to see whether they are doing the job right. Do agree with them the mechanism for feeding back – a meeting, a report or whatever.

What Will They Feed Back?

Don't expect them to give a blow by blow account of what they have done; focus instead on the outcome. What facts or pieces of information will tell you how well the job has been done?

ORGANISE YOUR DELEGATING

Who can you delegate to?	What can you delegate to them?	How can you brief them?	How will they feed back?

Using Secretaries Properly

Not everybody has access to the services of a secretary and, indeed, secretaries are beginning to disappear in some high tech firms where everyone works on a VDU. However, even there people are employed to help (they may be called admin. assistants or something similar) so our notes on secretaries apply to all people employed in this type of helping job.

To make the most of secretaries:

● Delegate as much as you can to them. (For example, you don't need to draft every letter - explain the purpose of a letter and ask the secretary to compile it.)

● Don't expect secretaries to do things that will waste their time (like making coffee, running errands etc).

● Do offer secretaries the same staff training and development opportunities as are available to other members of staff.

● Do involve secretaries in meetings.

● Do brief secretaries fully and regularly; always give them reasons for doing things explaining as much about the job as possible – things like the relative importance of the job, relevant background, etc.

✎ HOW WELL DO YOU USE YOUR SECRETARY?

Do you ask your secretary to:

	Tick	
	Yes	No
take on responsibilities?		
help organise your time?		
draft letters for you?		
organise and run filing systems?		
make arrangements (e.g. travel) for you?		
sort out problems you haven't time to see to?		

Why not ask your secretary to check your answers for you? If you don't have a secretary, is there someone you could ask to do such things for you?

TEAMS, EFFECTIVE AND OTHERWISE

Much small-group working takes place in teams. MacGregor (*The Human Side of Enterprise*) says their effectiveness can be judged by:

● Atmosphere – should be informal, comfortable and relaxed.

● Discussion – there is a lot of discussion, everybody takes part, but it remains relevant to the task in hand.

● Task well understood – the objective of the group is well understood by its members and accepted by them.

● Presence of disagreement – the group can handle disagreement because they look at the reasons for it, seek to resolve it, don't pretend that it doesn't exist.

● Decisions by consent – decisions are reached by general agreement, so there is no hidden opposition and grumbling afterwards.

● Criticism is acceptable – constructive criticism directed at removing problems, rather than personal attack.

● People are open - they are free to express their feelings as well as their ideas.

● Clear assignments are made – when action is taken, everybody knows what is expected of them, what their tasks are.

● The chair does not dominate – the leadership of the group may even change from time to time as different group members have different things to offer.

● The group is self conscious – it will take time to stop and see how well it is doing and what is getting in the way.

WHAT GROUPS DO YOU WORK IN?

Take one (or more) of the groups you listed in the exercise 'What People Do You Work With?' (above). How effective is it (are they)?

Tick

	Yes	No
Is the atmosphere relaxed?		
Is discussion encouraged?		
Do the group members understand their task well?		
Is disagreement tolerated?		
Are decisions reached by agreement?		
Is criticism accepted?		
Are people open?		
Are clear assignments made?		
Does the chair dominate?		
Is the group conscious of itself – i.e. has it aired the topics that are in this checklist?		

If the answer to the last question is 'yes', the group can itself work on other issues where it may not be performing well. If it is 'no' then perhaps it needs to be reformed – is this possible?

MEETINGS

Many of us spend a lot of time in meetings. Very often we find them frustrating. Yet we all feel pleased with a good meeting: what are the criteria for achieving one?

Timing

One of the worst features of many meetings is that they don't run to time. Everyone involved should understand the expected timings and that they'll be taken seriously:

- don't allow too much time
- if you are circulating an agenda or notice of the meeting, include a note of when it will start and finish
- arrive promptly, start and finish promptly
- think about the time of day when you will hold meetings; if possible make use of some other activity such as lunch or going home to close the meeting - but do not hold meetings just after lunch when people may feel sleepy.

On the other hand, plenty of time is needed for people who don't know each other to get acquainted if meetings with strangers are to be effective. This means ideally having meetings where there is plenty of time for discussion. If there's no time for such a meeting, try to allow people to get to know each other beforehand.

Organisation

Meetings will move more smoothly if properly organised; apart from anything else, everyone will know what's expected:

- prepare an agenda
- circulate it sufficiently in advance (but not too early as people will then forget it) with any supporting papers
- don't have 'Any Other Business' on the agenda - insist on everything for discussion being notified in advance
- if possible, consider having an agenda of one item only
- have spare copies of all papers available at the meeting – someone will have forgotten their copies.

Chair

How a meeting is chaired is probably the key ingredient in making it run smoothly. If you are chairing a meeting:

- keep to the agenda
- don't discuss at length complex items that can be given to a sub group or working party to sort out
- don't discuss at all items that don't belong there- don't butt in, let people have their say, summarise, get the consensus
- be aware of reticent people wishing to make important points.

If you aren't chairing the meeting but someone else is doing so, badly, you could drop this list of points on their desk!

People

The other magic ingredient in successful meetings is the people taking part. Things to consider include:

- how the room is arranged. For example, can you sit round a table? It's a lot more comfortable socially, everyone can see everyone else and also have something to spread papers and write on
- if it is to be a very short meeting, can you all remain standing?
- should smoking be allowed? Don't just assume that it's acceptable without asking everyone else.

 A RECENT MEETING I WAS AT...

'I was recently at a meeting with a couple of colleagues and three people from another organisation, on their premises, to get to know them since we would be working together on the same patch. They just sat at their desks and gave us chairs lined up along the wall. There was no agenda and they just talked, at least their manager did, for three hours. I had switched off after an hour.'

Purpose

No meeting will work if it's not clear what its purpose is. Make a note of the aims of each of the meetings you have. For each meeting add a note of:

- its purpose (is it to make a decision, to share information, to get to know someone?)
- who initiated it?

- how many were present?
- its value (e.g. high, medium, low)?

If the meetings are held regularly, review their purpose. How necessary are they? Could they be combined with others involving the same staff? Could they be delegated to someone else?

 Here is a note of one manager's meetings. All of these were necessary but a lot of time could have been saved by delegation and combination.

ONE MANAGER'S MEETINGS

Meeting/Purpose	Who initiated meeting?	How many present?	Value
Salary review	Self	2	High
Visitor to discuss training & computer systems	Others	2	Low
Trade association, to discuss membership	Self	3	Medium
Visitor to discuss project overseas	Others	3	Medium
Discussion of report by systems analysts	Self	8	Medium
Consultant, graduate recruitment literature	Others	2	High
Rehearse presentation	Others	6	Medium
Information technology planning meeting	Others	8	High
Group managing director	Other	7	High

HOW GOOD ARE YOU AT MEETINGS?

If you're not sure of the answer, use this checklist to think about the next meeting you have.

How many of your meetings achieve something by:

- solving a problem?
- deciding a line of activity?
- adding anything to what is already known?

Before you speak at a meeting do you ask yourself:

- whether you have anything important to say?
- whether anyone wants to hear it?
- whether this is the time to say it?

Do your meetings:

- start on time?
- finish on time?

Do you leave meetings feeling:

- that was a waste of time?
- that was useful?

COMMUNICATIONS

Effective communication is essential to good working relationships. The quality of our communicating depends on choosing:

The Right Message, the Right Medium

The biggest communication problem is getting the right message across. Error creeps in because:

- we don't like to say things that might cause offence or imply criticism
- it's even harder to be critical to someone we work for
- we don't like to say things that might imply bad things about ourselves
- language isn't always as clear and precise as it could be.

However, different types of error happen in different media. The main media are:

- face-to-face
- phone
- writing (including telex, computer).

 IN YOUR EXPERIENCE...

From your own experience, can you identify some problems caused by bad communication?

In what medium did they occur?

Would the bad communication have been less likely if a different medium had been used?

Face-to-Face

Choose this powerful form of communication if difficult things need to be said. However, you may be misunderstood if:

- you are giving the wrong non-verbal cues
- the recipient isn't listening or is distracted
- you tell them in the wrong place (in the canteen for example)
- they don't have something to make a note with
- the message is too complicated.

Let's spend a few minutes looking at the first two points on this list.

Non-verbal cues

A non-verbal cue is a gesture and expression that discloses attitudes and feelings. We give below a checklist of some of the commonest. You can use these:

- to gain a better understanding of what others are really saying to you
- to ensure that you convey exactly what you intend to when face-to-face with others.

Remember though, that it's not enough simply to *know about* correct communication techniques. Your aim should be to *employ* these techniques to enhance your message.

82

CUE CHECKLIST

Non-verbal cues	Possible processes
Furrowed forehead, knitted brows.	Thinking, rehearsing in an internal dialogue; giving self a bad time.
Tapping foot and/or drumming fingers.	Impatience; irritation; anger; agitation.
Avoiding eye contact.	Discomfort; anxiety; suspicion; confusion.
Intense eye contact.	Anger; concern; sexual attraction.
Rapid, light breathing.	Anxiety; fear; distress.
Irregular breathing.	Approaching an important issue; forcing self; controlling feelings.
Deep, slow breathing.	Supporting strong feelings - often precedes catharsis.
Physical stroking of face, arms and neck.	Comforting self *or* holding back from stroking others *or* holding back the need for comforting.
Scratching, pinching, gouging, severe pressing.	Punishing self, reflecting self-criticism or holding back from provoking or punishing someone else.
Controlled, low, quiet voice.	Suppressing energy/interest; excitement.
Fast, high voice.	Excitement; tension; fear.
Tightness/rigidity in jaw, neck, shoulder.	Holding back anger, sadness.
Clenching fists, tightness in arms.	Holding back anger, sadness.
Body leaning forward in chair.	Interested; concerned; about to 'happen'.
Body leaning backward in chair, sprawling.	Detached; uninvolved; unconcerned.
Arms tightly folded; legs tightly crossed.	Defending; putting up barriers; resistance.
Lounging extravagantly in the chair.	Detachment; cynicism; discounting.
Hand covering mouth.	Hiding; playing games; uncertain.
Finger jabbing.	Critical; putting down; fencing with.

Listening

Face-to-face communication needs active listening; this is one of the most neglected but crucial of management skills. Listening involves:

- hearing the message
- understanding it
- evaluating it – what does it mean?
- responding.

Responding is the overall aim of listening so poor listening is quite likely to lead to a weak or inappropriate response.

You can listen more actively to what someone is saying by asking yourself:

- why are they communicating – to give me information, to release some pent-up emotion, to develop a relationship with me, to persuade me of something?
- what are they trying to say?
- are they saying something I need to respond to?
- are they providing any non-verbal clues to what they are trying to say?
- can I help them if they are finding it difficult to express what they want to say by for example asking questions, indicating my interest in what they say and so on?

How often do you find yourself engaging in the 10 bad listening habits on page 85?
First, check the appropriate columns. Then tabulate your score using the key below.

For every 'Almost Always' checked, give yourself a score of	2
For every 'Usually' checked, give yourself a score of	4
For every 'Sometimes' checked, give yourself a score of	6
For every 'Seldom' checked, give yourself a score of	8
For every 'Almost Never' checked, give yourself a score of	10

Listening Habit	Frequency				
	Almost Always	Usually	Some-times	Seldom	Almost Never
1. Calling the subject uninteresting					
2. Criticising the speaker's delivery or mannerisms					
3. Getting *over*-stimulated by something the speaker says					
4. Listening primarily for facts					
5. Trying to outline everything					
6. Faking attention to the speaker					
7. Allowing interfering distractions					
8. Avoiding difficult material					
9. Letting emotion-laden words arouse personal antagonism					
10. Wasting the advantage of thought speed (day-dreaming)					
				Score	

Here are ten key ways in which you can improve your listening skills. You won't develop into a perfect listener overnight, but you'll certainly be able to improve your performance by reminding yourself regularly of these ten points.

Keys to Effective Listening	The Bad Listener	The Good Listener
Find areas of interest	Tunes out dry subjects	Opportunist; asks 'what's in it for me?'
Judge content, not delivery	Tunes out if delivery is poor	Judges content, skips delivery errors
Hold your fire	Tends to enter into argument	Doesn't judge until comprehension complete
Listen for ideas	Listens for facts	Listens for central themes
Be flexible	Takes intensive notes using only one system	Takes fewer notes. Uses 4-5 different systems depending on speaker
Work at listening	Shows no energy output. Attention is faked	Works hard, exhibits active body state
Resist distractions	Distracted easily	Fights or avoids distractions, tolerates bad habits, knows how to concentrate
Exercise your mind	Resists difficult expository material; seeks light, recreational material	Uses heavier material as exercise for the mind
Keep your mind open	Reacts to emotional words	Interprets colour words; does not get hung up on them
Capitalise on the fact that *thought* is *faster* than speech	Tends to daydream with slow speakers	Challenges, anticipates, mentally summarises weighs the evidence, listens between the lines to tone of voice

Phoning

This has most of the advantages and disadvantages of face-to-face communication except that you cannot see each other:

● if information is discussed or received from a phone call, make sure that you write a note with the date and time of the call.

● keep a pad and pencil handy by the phone – one message per sheet. Some offices use a standard message form for this purpose. If there's no follow-up letter this message may need to be filed and may have the same status as a letter.

● date all messages.

Writing

Much communication *has* to be in writing:

● if you're writing something which is circulated regularly, you might use a standard format for it; this gives people an immediate clue to what the information is - for example if it's the agenda for the weekly sales meeting, or the report of the last week's production

● remember to date all communications

● think about the purpose of a piece of writing before setting pen to paper

● think about the appropriate form of writing for your purpose (what level of polish for example)

● if it's important write a draft first, then edit it and polish it up before writing the final version

● if it's important, you're not sure whether your version is good enough, or you don't know how to make it say what you want it to say, get someone else to read it or listen to it – two minds are often better than one when it comes to writing.

WHAT'S THE RIGHT MEDIUM FOR THESE SITUATIONS?

(a) You want to reprimand a member of staff.
(b) You want to complain to a manager.
(c) You want to ask the research department for some information.
(d) You want to complain to a supplier about the non-delivery of some materials.
(e) You have to explain your company organisation to a group of visitors.
(f) You have to explain your development plan to a group of managers.
(g) You want to ask the council for a rates reduction on your premises.
(h) A member of staff has asked for advice on further training.
(i) You want to brief a colleague about a complex meeting next week.
(j) You want items for the agenda of the weekly production meeting from colleagues.

There isn't one right answer; some may have several.
Consider them in the light of the points above.
You might like to discuss them with colleagues or your mentor.

 Values at Work

A new bloke started work in our office recently. I came in one morning and found he'd stuck this notice on his desk:

> Leisure is secular, work is sacred. The object of leisure is work; the object of work is holiness.

I nearly blew a fuse. What business is it of his to tell me what to believe? Personally, I find leisure very enjoyable.

You may not have come across anything as extreme as this but you can probably think of instances in your own work where colleagues have put your back up because they hold different *values* to you. The topic of values can become very complex and we won't go into it in depth here. However, it's worth being aware of ways in which we can minimise conflict without necessarily compromising what we believe in. If you hold strong views on sex, politics or religion

- avoid 'telling' people. A relaxed discussion over lunch is far preferable to outburst and slogans

- put a premium on getting to know people *as* people rather than labelling them as opponents

- take things slowly. Avoid broadcasting your views with unfamiliar people or at an early stage in a new job.

Of course, you may not find yourself in this position. But however moderate you feel you are you're bound to come across people whose views or behaviour differ radically from your own. The important thing here is to admit these differences to yourself. It is usually unacknowledged conflict that subverts constructive discussion and prevents us getting on with the job in hand.

Next time you find yourself in disagreement with someone ask yourself: am I letting personal values influence my reaction to them? Do they differ from me in their:

- dress
- domestic life
- politics
- religious beliefs
- sexual preferences
- vocabulary
- race
- disabilities
- personal habits
- social status

If your answer to any of these points is 'yes' look very carefully at the basis for your disagreement; resist the temptation to let value differences colour your reactions. In fact, you'll be much less likely to do this once you have become conscious of possible areas of conflict.

 Have You Met Your Objectives?

Now that you have worked through this chapter, check back to the list of objectives that we gave at the start. Have you achieved all that you set out to?

WHAT NEXT?

 Your Agenda for Action

What else do you intend to do now?

● Are you planning to improve the way meetings are handled?

● Wil you delegate more work?

● Are you planning to develop your communication skills?

Elsewhere in the Book

Chapter 1 is about your job and that necessarily includes other people's views about it.

Chapter 2 is about time management and so about what you are going to ask other people to do for you and what demands they will be making of you.

Chapter 3 is about your problems, which are often caused by other people.

Chapter 6 is about where and how you keep things, important if they also want to use your tools or information.

Chapter 8 is about stress; other people can help handle it as well as sometimes causing it.

Help at Work

Training you could look for might include:

- listening – there may not be courses in listening as such but courses in, for example, counselling will help develop listening skills
- effective talking which will often cover aspects such as public speaking, managing meetings, etc. Video is a useful tool in practising your talking skills
- writing; as well as any courses on writing at work (such as report writing) you will find a lot of classes in adult education institutes, further education colleges and elsewhere, ranging from adult literacy (which covers many things – improving your spelling for example) to creative writing, writing for special purposes and many others
- running meetings.

6: FOR EVERYTHING, A PLACE...

 After reading this chapter you will be able to:
- explain the importance of storing things systematically
- organise the things you use at work
- find things when you need them.

INTRODUCTION

Can you find things when you want them? Most of us know someone whose tools are all over the place or whose desk is covered by heaps of paper yet we would be horrified if the books in a library were in heaps on the floor rather than arranged in order on the shelves. That's because we expect to be able to find what we want in a library while a heap of tools or pile of papers represents a personal and private area where we feel we *can* find anything when we need it.

The fact of the matter is, of course, that a library is a good example of how we should all keep our tools, materials and information, not only so that we can find them when we need them but to allow us to work efficiently in the meantime.

Can you find things?

THE COKE SACK

When I used to work as a maintenance engineer on the telephone system we often had to work at the side of the road and it was easy to get our tools lost in the grass. We used to take a coke sack and spread it out and then we'd arrange our tools on this sack so that we didn't lose them and we could lay our hand on the right tool straight away. It's the same as when you're changing the wheel on your car – you put the wheel nuts in the hub cap – if you don't you're pretty sure to lose one!

The principles used in running a library, namely the systematic storage of information, with ways of finding it when it's needed, apply just as much to the things we use in our own work. This applies to:

- a toolbox
- a desktop
- a small information system run by ourselves for our own needs
- a storage area for materials or components
- in fact just about anything where you have more than one item to handle!

We want such a system set up so that:

- we can find things when we want them
- we can find things quickly
- others can find things if we are off sick
- we know we've got the things we need
- we know they are being kept safely
- we can forget about them when we don't want them!

To ensure that a system achieves these aims:

● THE ITEMS MUST BE PUT INTO THE SYSTEM

● THEY MUST BE STORED IN AN ORGANISED WAY

● THERE MUST BE A METHOD FOR FINDING THINGS AGAIN WHEN WE WANT THEM

This sytem can be shown by a simple diagram:

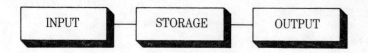

A SYSTEMATIC APPROACH

There are a few basic principles of organisation that will help you to work more effectively:

● Use systems that are as simple as possible, needing little more to operate them than common sense and the language you already possess – not complex classification systems (which you will end up not using).

● Use separate systems for things that are clearly different but do not devise any more systems than are absolutely necessary, otherwise you'll need an information retrieval system just to find your way round your information system!

● Organise systems so that anyone who might want to use them can understand them; for example a diary is a good system because it uses the calendar – a basic classification system which everyone is already familiar with.

But whatever system you select you'll still need to use it skillfully - you can't expect it to run itself. A system is only as good as the person who uses it!

 HOW DO YOU STORE THINGS AT PRESENT?

Next time you are in your work-area take a critical look at it. Ask yourself:

• What things do you have to keep in the course of your work?

• Where do you store them?

• How do you organise them?

• Could anyone work out how to find things if you weren't there?

WHAT TO COLLECT

It is easy to be swamped by paper so a useful rule is only to collect what is *essential* for doing your job. Check rigorously whether *you* must keep that item, whether someone else could keep it for you and whether it's really necessary to keep it at all.

You should be able to thin down the things you keep yourself to information, equipment, tools and materials (or components) that are absolutely basic to your daily work. Your basic needs may be little more than the personal information you need to do your job such as an address book or contact book, a diary or work schedule and... what else?

Who Else Can Help?

There are specialist departments in most organisations to help with storing things you need. This may be a library, a store, a central filing system, an information department and so on. Even if they don't exist, there are often such facilities outside the company which might offer some of the same services, sometimes for a charge, sometimes free!

- Is there a library in your organisation; do they keep the journals you also have on your shelf, do they keep cuttings from newspapers and journals, do they keep briefing files on topics of concern to the organisation?

- Are there other external information services which can provide similar facilities - local or specialist libraries, professional or trade organisations, cuttings services etc? Even if there is a charge involved it may be small compared with the cost of you storing your own information.

- Is there a central filing system in your organisation? If there is (and it works!), do you need to keep copies of all correspondence and reports? Such a system may be company wide, just operate at your site, just operate in your department. If one doesn't exist, is there anything to be gained by setting one up?

- Is there a central store? Do they have the things you need? They might well be more up-to-date than you about new materials, tools, pieces of equipment and so on.

If you do use other people for storing things you will of course have to find out what they offer, plan your work ahead, think about information you will need during each week, think about getting things from them regularly - but then if you are working effectively, you will be doing this anyway. Moreover, you should save plenty of time, part of which you can use for planning instead.

WHO CAN HELP AT YOUR WORKPLACE?

Do you have access to:	Yes	No	If Yes, is there anything they could do that you do at present?
a library?			
an information service?			
a central filing system?			
a central store?			
other central facilities?			
any such *public* or nationally available services?			

What Do You Collect?

You will still need to collect some things. This will probably include items such as addresses, appointments, times of meetings and notes of commitments – but other things will obviously vary from job to job.

✎ WHAT DO YOU NEED TO COLLECT?

Make a list of the types of information you collect regularly. Note against each item whether or not you *need* to collect that item yourself and if not, who else could collect it for you.

1. *Things you collect*	2. *Do you need to?*	3. *Who else could collect it?*	4. *(left blank for later use)*

STORING THINGS

What Do You Store at Present?

You have just noted the information that you *collect* – how much of it do you need to *keep*? The fac that you collect information and other things does not mean that you need to keep them as well. I there is someone else collecting it, they are also likely to have properly run storage systems.

If you store it yourself you will have to think about:

- hardware
- software
- updating.

Don't forget that here we are only talking about our *personal* systems; if information systems are needed for specialist jobs such as market research, then specialist systems wil probably be devised and specialist staff employed to manage them. If such specialist staff are employed they may well be able to help you with the organisation of your personal information system as well!

Keep only one piece of information on your desk or in front of you at a time. Everything else should be filed, in a pending tray or file, or otherwise stored.

That even means pencils and other things you need to have immediately to hand. Can you put your hand immediately on a pencil if you need one? And what about a pencil sharpener? A pencil pot or tray is a storage system too.

 ## WHAT DO YOU NEED TO KEEP?

Against the list of things that you need to collect (above), add a note in column 4 of the things you need to *keep* as well. That will provide you with a list of the things you need to store – to have immediately to hand.

DIFFERENT SORTS OF STORAGE

Hardware

This means the physical equipment used for storage. It could mean cupboards, filing cabinets, drawers, files, magazine boxes and lever arch files that can be kept on a shelf, a shelf itself if it's books that you're storing, a computer and so on.

Again, the keynote is simplicity. If a shelf and box files will suffice and will fit in your room – use them.

As your needs get more complex so too will your storage requirements and you may need to ask for specialist advice; for example, what is the best way of storing a map, a photographic negative, computer discs, samples of particular chemicals? If you have to store something you're not sure about ask your library, stationery department, works engineer or a technical specialist who should know.

What About Computers?

If you haven't come to terms with computers yet, you should think seriously about doing so. Familiarity with what computers can do will not only enhance your career potential, it is quite likely to help you in your immediate work.

Software

This means classification systems and the way you have organised things. The ideal classification system for the purpose is the one that works, that is simple, and that anyone can use. This may mean an alphabetical list of names, spare parts, topics, contacts, etc.

The best person to devise the system is the person who is going to use it; however, if several people are going to be using it, spend the necessary time discussing it so that you all understand the system and agree that you will use it.

Updating

An often overlooked issue is how you get rid of old, surplus or redundant information. Because things that are in a system are safely stored away, they can easily be forgotten. The waste paper basket is an invaluable storage aid!

 HARDWARE CHECKLIST

● Make a list of the things you require from a system:
for example:

1. must allow me to see the information without getting it out

2. must be dustproof

3. must be lightproof

4. must be able to hold things sized ___ by ___

5.

6.

7.

8.

9.

10.

Use another sheet of paper for futher notes.

● Identify a storage system that will meet each of these needs.

1. _____

2. _____

3. _____

4. _____

5. _____

6. _____

7. _____

8. _____

9. _____

10. _____

Use another sheet of paper for further notes.

● Which parts of your current system work at less than optimum efficiency?

● If you cannot work out what systems to use, or need advice about your current system, who can you ask?

 Have You Met Your Objectives?

Now that you have worked through this chapter check back to the list of objectives that we gave at the start. Have you achieved all that you set out to?

WHAT NEXT?

 Your Agenda for Action

What else do you intend to do now?

● Are you going to reorganise any parts of your system?

● Do you need help with any aspects of your storage system?

● Are there any skills you need to learn?

Elsewhere in the Book

Chapter 2 is about time management and this is directly related to the efficiency of your storage systems.

Chapter 4 is about your workplace and part of that is how you store things.

Chapter 5 is about working with people; you'll probably get on better with them if you can find the things they need as well as the things you need!

Chapter 7 is about handling change, something that's easier to do if we have some idea where we are now.

Chapter 8 is about switching off; you can do that more effectively if you can file away your work at the appropriate time.

Help at Work

Help with systems should be available from your library, information department, works engineers and so on.

There should be information available in-company from management services or the computer department about using information technology; there is also a lot of training available in using computers, from computer companies, in-company, and outside in the education and training system.

7: COPING WITH CHANGE

 After reading this chapter you will be able to:

- identify the changes that are happening which affect the way we work
- consider the key changes in your own work
- make some changes yourself.

INTRODUCTION

We're beginning to get used to the idea that change is a regular feature of life in the last part of the century. Some of us have already experienced a lot of change, others only a little, but it's certainly happening.

The most dramatic change has been the introduction of computer technology, which now affects most industries, even if it does not yet affect your own job directly. It is not the only change that's occurring however. Others include:

Technological changes: other technological changes include automation and the development of new materials and processes – the building industry, for example, has been affected dramatically by the use of plastics.

The international economy: we are part of a world economy now and what happens elsewhere affects us whether we like it or not. For example, oil prices have affected all countries, exchange rates affect our international competitiveness, EEC agreements have affected the fishing industry, and competition from countries with lower labour costs means that they can produce certain goods more cheaply than us (textiles for example).

The economy: we have become familiar with ups and downs in the British economy – in fact they have always happened. At present, along with many industrial countries, we are in the middle of a steady long-term growth in unemployment and we are also seeing the decline of older industries like shipbuilding and the development of new ones.

Business organisation: there has been a steady growth in the size of companies as the successful ones grow and amalgamate with others, and as large companies operate more and more on an international scale.

101

● Business methods: new ways of doing things have also developed with industry using new system and methods which often encourage flexibility, involvement and responsibility for their own wor from the workforce.

● Expectations and values: we ourselves have changed too in that we have higher expectations tha in the past. We expect a higher living standard, we expect to be involved more in decisions affectin our work and so on.

 ## WHAT CHANGES HAVE YOU SEEN?

What are the main changes that you have seen during your working life?

Which of them were due to technological change?

Which of them were due to changes in company structure and organisation?

Were any of them due to economic factors?

Were any of them due to other factors?

Did you cause any of the changes yourself?

Most of these are long-term changes whose impact is also long-term. Their implications for our wor and jobs are however clear:

● We will all need to update our skills regularly and develop new ones during our working life.

● We can't expect to work in the same job for such long periods as in the past; changing productic processes require different jobs.

● We all need to be adaptable, versatile and able to transfer our skills to different jobs.

● There is a possibility of different methods of working all of which suggest greater flexibility. F example, there is a growth in part-time work, working from home, job sharing and self employmen

We all need to be adaptable...

How Should We Respond?

We can respond to these changes by sitting waiting for them to happen, being fatalistic and saying there's nothing we can do about them, leaving them to happen to *us*.

Alternatively, we can take a positive approach to change both within our job and between jobs, expect to happen, be prepared for it and indeed help to make the changes happen ourselves.

The key skills in handling change well are:

- RESPONDING TO CHANGES THAT HAPPEN
- LEADING CHANGE OURSELVES IF WE CAN.

HANDLING CHANGE

Predicting it

We can't always know and understand everything that's happening around us; things are too comp
We can still be *aware* of change.

For example, we have known that computers were on the way for the last twenty years or more
know they're going to continue to make an impact on our lives. But there are still many people
ignore computers because they haven't yet affected their immediate job.

 IF COMPUTERS WORRY YOU...

Have you used a computer:

- at work?

- at home?

- elsewhere?

If your answer to each of these questions is 'no' we strongly recommend you to try out
computer for yourself. Most companies have computers available for employees who want som
basic familiarisation. Many run training courses. Failing that, you may very well find a loca
evening class can provide what you need.

If you answered 'yes' to any of the questions but are still worried, what else could you learn
explore? Consider:

- talking to someone in your own field who already uses a computer

- pinpointing exactly *what* your worry is. This may enable you to identify ways of coping wit
  your unease, for example, by further familiarisation. Even if you still find yourself unable
  like computers there's no reason why this should stop you using just those facilities that ca
  benefit your job.

It's possible to make intelligent guesses at directions in which things will develop and to respond accordingly.

We can look at possible changes through different timescales (short term, medium term, long term) and how these affect:

- the firm or industry we work in- our job specification – the things we have to do in our job and might have to do in the future

- our 'toolkit' – the skills and knowledge we use in our work and that we will need to continue to update to be effective in our work (and indeed our life).

 # WHAT CHANGES CAN YOU PREDICT?

Earlier, we asked you 'What changes have you seen?'
We would now like you to think ahead, to try to predict changes that might happen. This is obviously more difficult than looking backwards but here are some points that might help:

- Referring back to the changes you have experienced, did you expect them to happen?

- If not were there any clues around which could have helped you to expect them?

- Will they lead to any other further changes?

- Are there people you could talk to or is there company information you could read which would help you predict any areas in which future changes might happen?

- It's sometimes easier to see things that affect other people more clearly than things that affect ourselves. Can you see things happening to people you know (at your workplace or outside it) that might suggest changes that are going to happen?

Being Flexible

Being flexible is largely a state of mind – it's about how willing we are to change, to try new things, to be willing to accept that things (all sorts of things) won't always be the way they are.

For example, at times of war many people are willing to do things they wouldn't normally do – out of sheer necessity; in the First World War, women were suddenly acceptable as workers in many fields where they had previously not been.

HOW FLEXIBLE ARE YOU?

Answer the following questions as they apply to you. There is no right or wrong answer, so try to be as honest with yourself as you can.

During the last year, have you:

1. Visited one town or city that you have always wanted to visit but never have?

2. Tried out a new food or drink?

3. Read at least six books (half fiction, half non-fiction)?

4. Applied for a new job or taken on extra responsibilities in your present job?

5. Learnt a new skill (driving, horseback riding, pottery, billiards, badminton, French, windsurfing, etc.)?

6. Given up smoking, drinking or gone on a diet to lose weight?

7. Taken on a greater financial commitment requiring borrowing from a bank, finance house or friend?

8. Learnt a new word or expression you didn't know the meaning of before?

9. Met at least two new people who are now your friends?

10. Spent a considerable amount (say at least $50) on a pure luxury for yourself.

11. Tried a new type of holiday or work break (e.g. cycling, painting, adventure camping, 'Go as You Please')?

12. Been 'open' enough to tell someone the truth about themselves?

13. Met someone who has attracted you very deeply (emotionally, mentally, sexually)?

14. Seen one premiere of a play or film?

Can you add other statements to describe things that have happened to you and that you believe have stretched you?

'Yes' answers indicate flexibility and 'no' answers indicate lack of inclination to change or try new things but you shouldn't expect to score at the extremes of all 'Yeses' or all 'Noes'. However, the biggest value of this exercise is not so much to score yourself as to provide an opportunity to think about yourself – are you as flexible as you would like to be?

We can also develop specific skills to help us to act in a flexible way and this is discussed in the next section.

ENCOURAGING CHANGE

Yourself

Trainers frequently break down training topics into attitudes, skills and knowledge. This is certainly a useful way of looking at what is involved in change.

Attitudes

We have already discussed an attitude that helps us to cope with change, namely flexibility. However, change can also bring uncertainty and for many people this is a cause of anxiety and even stress.

The main thing we can do to cope with anxiety is to recognise that it exists; that in itself can remove some of the pressure and also allows us to start dealing with it. If we recognise it, we can then try to understand its causes and whether there are things that we can do about them.

 DOES CHANGE CAUSE YOU ANXIETY?

Answer each of the following questions as honestly as you can:

1. Are there some things that worry you about changes?

2. Did the changes you identified above cause you anxiety?

3. How did you handle them?

4. Could you have handled them better?

5. Is there anybody you could have talked to to help you handle them better?

If you answered 'yes' to 1 or 2 you'll find the next chapter, on handling stress, of value.

Skills and Knowledge

We learn things at work, during education and training, when we watch TV, when we read, in fact all the time. However, you can structure your learning so that you learn things that you want to or that will be useful to you.

We can use education or training for many things:

- to learn a new skill or knowledge

- to update an existing skill

- to gain *extra* skills to enhance those you already have (e.g. management skills, writing skills, marketing, applications of computers)

- to gain a qualification in order to validate a skill that you have already acquired by yourself

- to try out or test a field that you are interested in but are not sure about

- to take a structured look at your work and at ways of developing it.

Here is a simple set of questions that you can ask yourself to help identify things you need to learn

- Where am I now? (i.e. in work or life – this may well relate to some of the things you wrote down in Chapter 1)

- Where would I like to be? (it may be helpful to add – in 1 year, 5 years, 10 years etc.)

- What will I need to get there? (that could well be knowledge and skills but could also be attitude changes or experience; acquiring those is also learning)

- Have I got these things? If not, how can I get them? (and this will lead directly into the types o education and training you might like to use).

There is information on how to find out more about education and training at the end of the chapter

Your Job

Is there scope for development in your job? You may have got ideas about this from the other chapters in the book but you may equally like to think about this now.

YOUR JOB – A CHECKLIST

Are there any features of your job where development is possible? If so list them.

Who can you talk to in order to progress these ideas? Why not use your adviser for an initial, informal chat?

If you have no ideas, who can you talk to in order to try and create some? (There are very few jobs where no development at all is possible.)

 Have You Met Your Objectives?

Now that you have worked through this chapter check back to the list of objectives that we gave at the start. Have you achieved all that you set out to?

- Have you understood the changes that are happening which affect the way you work?
- Have you thought about changes in your own work- do you know how you might make some changes yourself?

WHAT NEXT?

 Your Agenda for Action

What else do you intend to do now?

● Do you intend to work on any of your attitudes or anxieties?

● Do you intend to try and learn anything new?

● Do you intend to try to make any changes in your working situation or job?

Elsewhere in the Book

Chapter 1 is about your job and therefore highly relevant to changes you might think of making.

Chapter 2 is about time management; are there changes in your use of time that would be beneficial?

Chapter 3 is about problem solving; some problems arise out of change - equally change could be the solution to some problems.

Chapter 4 is about your workplace and how it affects your work – changes there can equally enhance your work.

Chapter 5 is about people, one of the most changing elements in any work situation.

Chapter 8 is about switching off, handling the stresses of work, and also of change.

Help at Work

The problem with education and training is that there is so much of it, how do we find what is right for us?

At work, try your training department or the open learning unit, if you have one.

If you want to find out about training outside work there is a useful guide called *Second Chances for Adults* which lists and describes all the education and training opportunities in the country available to people tho have left school. More details in the *Suggested Reading*.

8: SWITCHING OFF

After reading this chapter you will be able to:

- pinpoint the sources of stress in your work
- organise your work so that you can minimise stress
- prepare a plan to lead a less stressful life
- switch off!

INTRODUCTION

The idea of 'stress' conjures up a picture of someone suffering from overwork or other pressure but this is not the whole picture.

To start with, *stress* itself is not harmful but it is the *side effects* of too much stress which may well lead to illness.

One of the biggest sources of stress is unfinished work.

Stress can also be beneficial by helping us to do difficult things; actors and musicians are often nervous before performing, sportsmen and women have to build up a winning frame of mind if they are to excel and in handling difficult jobs we too may need extra nervous tension to enable us to get started and to work through to a successful conclusion. It is only when stress is too great or lasts too long that it becomes harmful.

In previous chapters we have looked at ways of making work more routine inorder to reduce stress. This chapter, however, is concerned with the effects of too much stress, the bad effects it can have and how to regulate it. In particular it looks at:

● HOW TO PLAN YOUR WORK AND LIFE SO AS TO AVOID UNNECESSARY STRESS

● HOW TO DEAL WITH TOO MUCH STRESS IF IT HAPPENS.

DO YOU WORK TOO MUCH?

Tick

		Yes	No
1.	Are you often late for appointments?		
2.	Do you often forget things?		
3.	Do you eat while working?		
4.	Do you think present work problems are temporary and that things will soon be OK?		
5.	Do you often find yourself talking about work on social occasions?		
6.	Are all your friends connected with work?		
7.	Do you think about work last thing at night and first thing in the morning?		
8.	Do you regularly wake up in the night thinking about work?		
9.	Are you still thinking about work when you get home in the evening?		
10.	Do you take work home with you regularly?		

DO YOU WORK TOO MUCH?

These are some of the symptoms of overwork. If you have answered 'yes' to many of them then you should take a break to think about the way you organise your work. If you didn't answer 'yes' to many of them you can still use them as an early warning system – if you find your behaviour changing in several of these areas, regard this as a danger signal and do something about it.

One of the biggest sources of stress is unfinished work. It's not possible to work 24 hours a day, seven days a week and still be effective. We all have a finite amount of time within which we can work well and it's more important to use that time well than to try to work more hours.

Ways of using your time better are discussed in Chapter 2.

HANDLING STRESS

Identifying It

What are the symptoms of stress? They may be physical, or to do with your behaviour and feelings. For example:

Physical Symptoms

Trembling, twitching, an increased pulse rate, hot and cold spells, feeling sick, tension, tense stomach - in fact any signs that your body is not at ease.

Behaviour

Having more accidents, being careless, snapping at people, being more aggressive when driving, not being able to sit still or settle down to a job, eating, drinking, smoking or taking drugs too much – more than you would normally.

Feelings

Feeling depressed, worried, alienated, panicky, sensitive to criticism and so on.

These are all symptoms of stress and since we may experience a few of them at any time, as when we are tired for example, they do not by themselves indicate anything to be alarmed about. If a number of them are present continuously for a period however that should be taken as a warning to at least stop and check whether there is something that needs putting right.

Defusing It

Many of the techniques described above for avoiding stress may also be useful ways of defusing it. However, there are ways to handle the immediate symptoms too.

Techniques

● Try to stop talking. Listen to other people instead. That means listen actively to what they are saying – don't finish their sentences for them, not even in your mind!

● If you feel yourself getting impatient or frustrated about situations where you have to wait, like in traffic or queues, ask yourself why you are allowing it to annoy you and then consciously try to relax.

● When you are feeling very stressed about something, stop, ask yourself will this matter in five days (or five months), must I do it now, can't it wait; what is the worst thing that can happen if I don't finish it?

● Above all, try to identify the source of tension, remove the source and relax the tension.

People

Having some good strong friendships is an important part of avoiding stress. Other people can also help you to deal with stress when it happens. When in a stressful situation, many people find it harder to talk about a problem so it's doubly important to have good relationships with people beforehand; good friends will insist on helping you when you need it - let them! In particular, other people can help by:

• providing someone to talk to
• providing information
• providing advice
• doing something for you.

High Stress Jobs

There are jobs where stress is unavoidable, perhaps because of the nature of the work, perhaps because of the working conditions. If you work in such a job, it may be necessary to limit the time you spend in that job; if that is the case you should plan how and when you will leave the job, even before you start it.

IS YOUR JOB A HIGH STRESS JOB?

If you don't know the answer to this question, you might like to keep a stress log for a few weeks. It could take the following form:

Date	Source of Stress	What effect did it have on you?	Could it have been avoided?

If you find that there are several sources of stress that affect you, very regularly, and that they cannot be avoided, you have probably got a high stress job.

Can you handle these stresses?

Will you be able to for five years?

Will you be able to for ten years?

How long will you be able to handle them before you need to change job?

Are there any preparations you should make so that you can change your job when you need to?

The Effects of Change

All changes cause a certain amount of stress, whether they are helpful or negative changes. For example, some of the changes that cause high stress in adults are:

- the death of a spouse or close family member

- divorce or separation (or getting together again after a separation)

- injury or illness

- marriage

- losing a job or changing a job

- retirement

- pregnancy

and so on.

Change is stressful because we have to adapt and adjust. It is more stressful if several changes are happening at the same time. As we discussed in Chapter 7, we have to adjust to many changes at work these days as well. We cannot usually stop changes happening but it's worth being aware that change has side effects so that we know that this is a time of higher risk. It's also sensible to try and avoid having several changes happen at the same time.

Your Individual Pattern

It is not only jobs that are stressful; we are individually more or less prone to stress because of factors such as:

- attitudes – do you think positively or do you always expect the worst?

- aptitudes – are there some things you do more easily than others?

- health – are you in a good state of health?

- physique – are you fit?

Whatever your own individual characteristics, allow for them.

WHAT ARE YOU LIKE?

Spend a few minutes answering the following list of questions as honestly as you can.

Are there things that are more difficult for you to do because of your physique?

Are there things that are difficult for you because of your health?

Do you make a habit of looking at things in a positive way?

Are there some things that you find easy to do?

Are there things you find difficult?

When you have answered each question, you may like to answer these two extra questions for each item:

- is this something that causes extra stress in your work?

- is this something that you can change in any way, either by changes in yourself or by changes in your work?

AVOIDING STRESS

We've already looked at ways of handling stress when it arises. But there are also ways of becoming less susceptible to stress. Let's take a look at these now.

Do you Lead a Balanced Life?

An important first step in avoiding stress is to make sure that the different parts of our life are balanced so that all the things that are important to us have their own space. No one area should have a bad effect on the others. If we can manage this it will have a good effect on all the areas concerned - detachment from our job can lead to it being done more effectively.

You must however, sort out your own personal priorities – each of us has a different balance of interests in our life. For example, how much time do you (and should you) allow for:

- work
- family
- friends
- leisure
- other things that are important to you?

WHAT ARE YOUR PRIORITIES?

What percentage of time do you think you should allow to each of:

- family
- work
- friends
- leisure
  (other things – list them)?
  -
  -
  -

Plot them on this chart; the line represents *all* your time. Mark on it the percentage of your time that you actually spend on each.

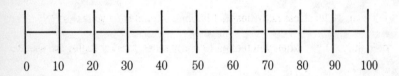

Now repeat the same diagram, only this time plotting how much time you should be allowing for each:

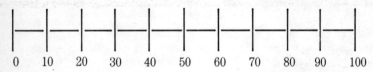

The results should speak for themselves!

When planning the balance – you should ask who you should be sharing this planning with - it will tell you a lot about your priorities. If you've allocated a greater importance to work and haven't discussed it with the family, this may suggest that they have a priority. Family is important to health and so too are good friendships.

118

A Well Balanced Day

On a different time scale it's also important to plan the balance of activities in each day well. This means both how much time you spend on activities of high and low stress and the order in which you perform them. In particular you should

- avoid monotony (if you are doing a job that will require a day (or days) of uninterrupted concentration on one task, make sure you have a five minute break every hour)
- do one job at a time
- plan variety into the day (have regular changes of activity, and of pace, preferably involving different types of work)
- have regular breaks – *do* use your lunch breaks.

There is a more detailed discussion of these issues in Chapter 2 p41.

What are the low and high stress activities that happen often during your work?

Are there some times of day when you feel particularly tense, tired or highly stressed?

How many breaks do you take in the day?

Can you use these different factors to help you plan what you should do when in the day?

Balanced Eating

Meals and eating are important for health and stress management. This not only includes *what* you eat but also *how* you eat. Some simple rules are:

- do have regular meal breaks
- don't keep eating between meals
- don't eat while you're working.

You may find too that you feel tired just before or just after a meal and so should not plan these as times of high activity.

Switching Off

There is no point having the balance in your life and your day well worked out if you are not able to switch properly from one to the other; boundaries between different areas are important. You must therefore decide at what point in the day your work stops and your private life starts. If you work at home, this is even more important. *How* can you decide?

● Decide that a particular point is the time you make the switch from work to home. For example, when you walk out of the office, when you get out of your car, when you have your evening meal - whatever features regularly in your life and signifies a change of pace, people and environment for you. Try to discipline yourself not to think about work after you have passed that point. You can use the same process in reverse when changing from home to work.

● Use your relaxation time to relax. Plan time for leisure and relaxation and use this for activities which are different from your work; for example, if you spend most of your time working on a VDU, don't spend all your leisure time watching television; if you spend most of the day sitting, do something physically active like cycling, swimming, gardening, cooking, etc.

● Do take the holiday time to which you are entitled and do have holidays.

● Many people use exercise or relaxation classes (like Yoga, Keep Fit, Aerobics) to help relax. This is fine but don't think that that is the only way of relaxing or keeping fit (though Yoga may well teach you some techniques for relaxing physically and mentally). Attending a carpentry class or playing golf or going to a local history class can all be equally useful ways of relaxing if they represent a change and exercise the parts of the body or mind that are ignored when you are working.

 HOW DO YOU SWITCH OFF?

How do you move from a home to a work phase and back again?

What are the things you do to relax?

Do you use any formal relaxation techniques?

When was your last holiday?

Did it provide a complete break?

When is your next holiday?

Physical Health

This is not a book on keeping fit, but being healthy is an important part of handling stress. There is now fairly wide agreement on certain basic rules for keeping healthy and these are:

- eat breakfast
- eat regular meals – no snacks in between, no junk food
- don't smoke, and if you do, at least try to reduce the amount you smoke
- have a balanced diet
- use alcohol only in moderation
- try not to be over or under weight for your height
- get enough sleep (seven to eight hours a night)
- get regular vigorous exercise (at least 20 minutes three times a week)
- have regular annual checkups, especially if you are over 40.

 Have You Met Your Objectives?

Now that you have worked through this chapter check back to the list of objectives that we gave at the start. Have you achieved all that you set out to?

WHAT NEXT?

 Your Agenda for Action

What else do you intend to do now?

- Can you identify things that cause stress at work that can also be changed? Who can help you change them?

- What activities will you add to your life to help you relax?

- Are there members of your family, friends or colleagues who are under stress and whom you could help?

Elsewhere in the Book

Chapter 1 is about your job – the accurate definition of goals is an important part of working with a minimum of stress.

Chapter 2 is about time, one of the biggest sources of stress; plan it better.

Chapter 3 is about problems; handle them so that they don't become stressful.

Chapter 4 is about your workplace and possible sources of stress such as bad heating, ventilation or lighting, pollution etc.

Chapter 5 is about people – get on better with them and you will reduce the stress in your life.

Chapter 6 is about finding things which will make everyday working life run more smoothly.

Chapter 7 is about change , a major source of stress because it is not acknowledged and dealt with appropriately.

Help at Work

If you have a stress problem at work, your manager should be able to help you. The personnel department or medical services may be able to help too. The training department may run courses on stress management.

BEAT STRESS AT WORK

Jacqueline Atkinson

Stress isn't harmful – it's the way we react to it that causes the problems. In this informative though non-technical volume **Jacqueline Atkinson** explains *** How to determine if you are stressed * Identifying the precise cause of your stress * The role of nutrition and exercise in general health * Adjusting mental attitudes to overcome stress *permanently!***
Thorsons Paperback   ISBN 0 7225 1485 9

THE HIGH FLIER'S HANDBOOK

William Davies

Two hundred or so ideas and concepts essential to anyone who aims to fly-high in the business world. If you act on just half a dozen of the entries you will improve efficiency and

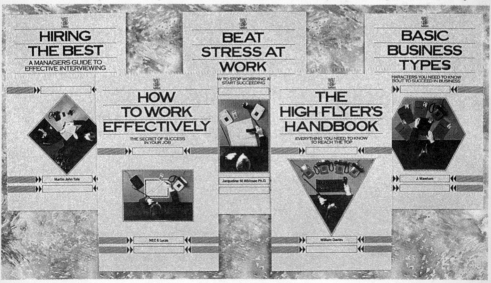

increase your chances of reaching the top.

Includes: persistence; planning; procrastination; word games – 'Rightly or wrongly' etc; plus much more.

Thorsons Paperback   ISBN 0 7225 1706 8

HIRING THE BEST

Martin John Yate

The essential guide for everyone charged with the tremendous responsibility of hiring company personnel. **Martin John Yate** demonstrates conversational and questioning techniques designed to reveal a candidate's strengths and weaknesses. Includes questions for managers, salespeople and recent graduates; shows how to define a departments needs; examines the entire interviewing process including shortlisting and telephone interviewing.

Thorsons Paperback   ISBN 0 7225 1733 5

BASIC BUSINESS TYPES

John Wareham

A thoroughly engrossing and satirical revelation – in a series of unforgettably wise, witty and sometimes even ribald profiles – of precisely who wins and who loses in the corporate business world . . . and why! Includes straight-to-the-point revelations about: *Emperor and Queen Bee, McCoy and more readily identifiable characters.*

Thorsons Paperback   ISBN 0 7225 1712 2